Gender in the
Workplace

A Case Study Approach

Jacqueline DeLaat

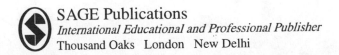

SAGE Publications
International Educational and Professional Publisher
Thousand Oaks London New Delhi

For information:

SAGE Publications, Inc.
2455 Teller Road
Thousand Oaks, California 91320
E-mail: order@sagepub.com

SAGE Publications Ltd.
6 Bonhill Street
London EC2A 4PU
United Kingdom

SAGE Publications India Pvt. Ltd.
M-32 Market
Greater Kailash I
New Delhi 110 048 India

Printed in the United States of America

Library of Congress Cataloging-in-Publication Data

DeLaat, Jacqueline.
    Gender in the workplace: A case study approach / by Jacqueline DeLaat.
       p. cm.
    Includes bibliographical references.
    ISBN 0-7619-1478-1 (acid-free paper)
    ISBN 0-7619-1479-X (acid-free paper)
     1. Sex discrimination in employment—United States—Case studies.
    2. Sex role in the work environment—United States—Case studies.
    I. Title.
    HD6060.5.U5 D45   1999
    306.3'615'0973—dc21   98-58080

This book is printed on acid-free paper.

99 00 01 02 03 04 05 7 6 5 4 3 2 1

Acquisition Editor:	Marquita Flemming
Editorial Assistant:	Mary Ann Vail
Production Editor:	Denise Santoyo
Editorial Assistant:	Patricia Zeman
Designer/Typesetter:	Lynn Miyata
Cover Designer:	Candice Harman

Gender in the Workplace

To Dora, Korey, Susan, Eileen . . .
who've shared the struggles . . .
and Meghan, Michelle, Ruth, and Leslie . . .
with hopes the struggles will ease.

Contents

Preface

Attention to gender issues in the workplace is heightening in the 1990s, as men and women confront new challenges and difficulties in achieving gender equity and fair treatment at work. Sexual harassment has dominated recent public interest, but other issues are also critical, such as the glass ceiling in advancement, sex stereotyping of certain categories of work, continued pay inequities between men and women, career development issues, and perhaps most important, problems in balancing family needs with the structure and demands of the workplace. Although most Americans accept the fairness of equal treatment for the genders in the workplace, few would argue that it has been achieved. Furthermore, the issues appear quite complex and intransigent, despite a number of public policies directed at workplace equality.

The purpose of the cases in this text is to raise awareness of the current forms gender issues in the workplace are taking and to encourage active thinking about how these issues may be addressed. Everyone who works or will soon work can benefit from the exercise. The material should prove useful to students in a variety of college courses related to management, business, public administration, personnel management, public policy, and gender studies, and also to a wide variety of people already confronting the issues in the workforce.

Acknowledgments

I thank the Faculty Development Committee of Marietta College for critical support at several key points in the development of these cases, and the Legal Education Fund of the American Bar Association for a supportive grant in the summer of 1997. Editor Marquita Flemming has my deep gratitude for her confidence in developing the project. Attorney Amy Wind provided invaluable help on the legal issues involved in the cases. Finally, the many professional women who have shared their stories also deserve credit for being the real "teachers" involved in this project.

Introduction

Faith Daniels, the NBC news correspondent, tells an interesting story about her first "real" job after college graduation. Having been treated fairly in every way as an undergraduate mass media major, she was an honors student, had been mentored by a very experienced faculty member, completed a prize internship in television, and entered the job market confidently. She interviewed for a news opening with a local television station and excitedly waited for the phone call to tell her she was hired. When the call came, however, the manager said, "Well, we're sorry but we don't think you would work out in news; however, we do have an opening for a 'weather bunny' and we think you'd be great at that!" "This was my first introduction to stereotyping of women at work," Ms. Daniels later told a group of undergraduate women, "and it shows the kind of attitudes and behaviors you may run into."

Many successful working women have similar tales to tell. Younger people, however, seem to believe that gender discrimination and its causes are things of the past. Although it is true that much progress toward work equity has been made in recent decades, there is substantial evidence that serious gender issues arise in many contemporary places of work. This brief collection of cases is designed to help students and employees to understand what some of these issues are and to confront them in the real-life situations presented in the case studies. Gender issues in the workplace are often subtle, difficult to address, and difficult to prepare students and workers to address. Yet many can expect to be confronted with gender discrimination in the course of their careers.

Most undergraduates, male and female, believe that gender inequality has been "solved" through public policy—legislation and court decisions—but are quite unaware of what the law actually addresses, what practices in the workplace it prohibits, and how the legal system adjudicates issues of gender and work. In addition, individual organizations and professions present unique variations of these gender issues, yet many young professionals seem totally unprepared for them. It is quite difficult for employees with very limited work experience to develop individual strategies for coping with gender issues at work, should they be required to do so. Greater understanding of these matters will greatly assist young professionals as they enter the workforce; such insights are also sought in many organizations and professional groups, through employee and management training programs addressed to gender issues. This text presents a brief overview of gender issues in the workplace, along with one representative case study for each category of these gender issues. Its format and content are suitable for both undergraduate students and organizational development training in work settings.

 Topics

The text begins with a brief exploration of the range and types of gender issues in the workplace, organized into five major categories:

1. *Gender stereotypes about work,* for example, "Women don't do lumber."

2. *Gender discrimination in compensation, promotion, and benefits,* that is, glass ceiling issues.

3. *Career development and mentoring.*

4. *Balancing work and family responsibilities,* that is, child care, dual-career couples, and pregnancy issues.

5. *Sexual harassment* issues.

Later in this introduction, I will define these five categories of issues and provide concrete examples of the issues in each category, chosen from a variety of current work environments. Relevant data and research on the issues will also be summarized, along with key definitions, some illustrative examples, and concepts. (The intent, however, is to provide a broad overview of these issues, useful in a variety of teaching settings, rather than an in-depth, specialized summary of the research, which is readily available elsewhere.) This material will familiarize students or trainees with the broad range of gender issues in the workplace and help bring order to this material by grouping issues in the above categories.

Each of the five subsequent chapters is a case study illustrating one particular category of gender issues. For example, Chapter 1 presents the case "Half a Pie, or None?" which focuses on gender stereotyping of certain positions within an organization. The cases are all based on real situations; several were drawn from federal court cases, whereas others were developed from personal interviews on the topics of the case. The Student Responses promote analysis and evaluation of information in the actual case, as well as present activities that may enhance learning from the case.

(Additional background information useful to discussion of the issues is provided in an important companion volume, the *Instructor's Notes.*)

I emphasize case studies here as an innovative teaching technique, well suited to the objectives of increasing awareness of how actual workers, both men and women, as well as the law and the legal system, address gender issues in the workplace. Both students and employees may have a very limited base of experience related to gender issues, and the use of case studies provides an effective way of increasing their ability to apply what they learn. Without concrete application, the study of gender issues can seem remote, indeed, especially to undergraduates. Traditional treatment of gender issues focuses on both the theory of gender and data or evidence that gender discrimination occurs. Although this work is very valuable, it tends to be rather theoretical. The use of some specific case studies, which engage learners more actively and directly in the issues at hand, makes the gender content of many undergraduate and graduate courses, as well as training on gender within work organizations, much more concrete. Case studies can thus extend the experience and perspective of students and/or employees who might not have encountered certain issues personally.

The case studies included here are based on actual legal cases, nationally reported incidents, or personal interviews, with names and some identifying details changed. The development of cases involves researching the legal issues, choosing a good illustrative case, writing the case in a story or scenario format, and developing key objectives and questions for analysis. In some case studies, classroom simulations may be used to recreate the circumstances presented in the case and allow student responses. In all cases, discussion questions focused on the critical events in the case encourage the students to think about the gender, legal, and managerial issues in a concrete situation, thus greatly enhancing classroom or training site discussion and participation.

Case studies place students directly "in the action," by requiring problem solving and personally developed responses to the situations presented in the case. For example, in a case about gender stereotyping of work, both supervisors and the individual being denied access to certain work have practical and legal options and responsibilities; the case includes activities that reflect both of these perspectives on the work situation. Case studies thus help to promote lively, active learning environments, in which most people can learn more readily than in a more passive environment.

The concluding chapter of this volume is devoted to an examination of the *connections* among the five categories of gender issues explored in the cases. For example, sexual stereotyping of work often leads to inequities in compensation or promotion. The importance of the organizational culture in gender issues at work is also highlighted in the concluding chapter. Students or trainees who complete all five cases will be able to compare the differences between organizations that affect both the nature of a gender issue and how it might be most effectively addressed. Solutions that are feasible in an academic environment, for example, may not be effective in the military due to differences in the nature, values, and mission or goals of the organizations involved. Consider, next, a brief introduction to each of the five categories of gender issues in the workplace.

Gender Stereotyping of Work

Regarding certain types or categories of work as "male" and others as "female" constitutes gender stereotyping of work. Industrial sociologists, among others, have studied such patterns in the U.S. workforce over time, and U.S. Census data about the gender composition of various professions and jobs provides the data for such analyses.

During the 1970s and 1980s, occupational sex segregation declined for the first time in the 20th century (Reskin & Padavic, 1994, p. 79). A variety of social and legal, as well as economic, factors contributed to this decline, including passage and initial enforcement of Title VII of the 1964 Civil Rights Act; the emergence of the second "women's movement" of the century in the 1970s; and increased educational opportunities for women resulting from other federal policies such as Title IX of the Education Amendments of 1972, which requires all educational institutions receiving federal money to treat men and women equally.

The numbers of women in many formerly male professions—notably law, medicine, government, and academia—have increased dramatically in this period. One of the most important contributing factors has been the increased similarity among men and women in the percentage graduating from college, in their college majors, and in their choice of postgraduate education. In 1960, 38% of all college graduates were female, but the percentage has risen steadily since then, and passed the 50% mark in the early 1980s. Only 3% of all professional degrees were granted to women in 1960, but by 1987 that percentage was 35%. Half of current law school graduates are female (Goldin, 1990).

However, it is also clear that sex segregation persists in the workforce. The stark occupational data confirm that women and men are still segregated into distinct careers, despite the reduction in the overall amount of such segregation in the past few decades. The ten most common occupations for women, according to 1990 census data, were (in order): secretary; elementary school teacher; cashier; registered nurse; bookkeeper; nurse's aide; salaried manager, administrator; sale representative; waitress; and salaried sales supervisor. For men, the list is as follows: salaried manager, administrator; truck driver; salaried sales supervisor; janitor; carpenter, apprentice; sales representative; construction laborer; cook; supervisor, production occupation; and automobile mechanic (U.S. Bureau of the Census, 1992). Furthermore, it is also clear that the occupations dominated by women are less compensated and less valued than those dominated by men (U.S. Bureau of Labor Statistics, 1992).

As Reskin and Padavic (1994) so ably summarize, this segregation persists because of a variety of factors: The actions of employers, actions of male workers, and actions of female workers all contribute to occupational segregation by gender. Although, as Goldin (1990) reports, most explicit rules prohibiting women from certain types of work or requiring them to resign on marriage are now illegal, the impact of these earlier practices remains. It is also correct that if "women's work" has been defined in one way, and "men's work" in another, few individuals may be willing to oppose that established pattern (Goldin, 1990, p. 8).

These social norms help perpetuate job segregation, even though it is illegal. Employers may discriminate intentionally or unintentionally, both of which, of course, violate Title VII. Recruitment practices, interviewing questions and techniques, and stereotypes of initial recruiters or "gatekeepers" can all operate to discriminate unfairly against one gender. Furthermore, requirements or skills qualifications may be unfair and operate against women or men; at times one sex is provided with better training opportunities denied to the other, which is also an unfair practice. Employers' control of workplace rules and structure (such as location and hours of work, shift rotations, etc.) may also operate to discourage women or men from entering a certain type of work.

In addition to employers' actions, one gender of co-workers may create an atmosphere or workplace dynamic that effectively excludes the other. For example, men often fear the entry of women into their profession for a variety of reasons, including the new competition, a decline in the prestige of the work, the need to "clean up" workplace behavior or language, or that women may not "do their share" (Reskin & Padavic, 1994, p. 72). Some men thus feel they have a stake in keeping women out of their work, and they act on this feeling. Of course, some of these actions may be illegal.

Women themselves may contribute to their occupational segregation. To the extent that women do not pursue careers they obviously cannot develop them. Although choices of men and women may "voluntarily" exclude them from a certain type of work, Reskin and Padavic's analysis—that such "free choice" is largely socially and organizationally determined—is compelling (p. 79). In the current era, for example, it is not clear that women do not seek similar careers and the same job satisfactions that men do; the numbers of women in the permanent workforce, and research about them, indicate the changes from previous eras in this regard (Jencks, Perman, & Rainwater, 1988). It is more likely that women modify their career objectives and choices because of a combination of socialization, role-conflict, and organizational and professional realities than from true free choice.

In the case "Half a Pie, or None?", issues of occupational segregation by gender are raised in the context of a highly trained, professional woman seeking career advancement to managerial levels. The case illustrates ways in which employer actions can lead to occupational segregation, in spite of the legal ban on such actions provided in Title VII. The actions of supervisors as well as co-workers, both male and female, are important in the case.

 ## Gender Discrimination in Compensation, Promotion, Benefits: The Glass Ceiling

A second area of gender discrimination in the workforce relates to compensation and advancement. Government and private research has authoritatively documented the "pay gap" in earnings between men and women; in 1992 women earned about 74 cents for each dollar earned by men (Karsten, 1994, p. 53). Part of the gap, of course, is related to the occupational segregation of women and the corresponding lower pay rates for "women's jobs."

However, there is also much discrepancy between the earnings of men and women even within the same occupation. Only about 7% of the gap, within certain occupations, can be accounted for by education and experience differences between men and women (U.S. Bureau of the Census, 1992). This tends to discredit the "pipeline theory," which has argued that women have not been "in the pipeline" long enough to gain the experience needed for top-level positions. (The larger numbers of women remaining in the workforce throughout their adult life also discredits the pipeline theory in the current context.)

As in cases of occupational segregation, there is significant national policy against unequal pay and related practices, in the Equal Pay Act of 1963. This was passed as an amendment to the Fair Labor Standards Act of 1938; it stipulates that men and women must be compensated equally for jobs that are alike in content; that require similar skill, effort, and responsibility; and are performed under similar working conditions. The act includes incentives and employee benefits as well as wages. Women and men may be paid different rates for doing the same work only based on a legitimated seniority or merit system. The act applies only to pay discrimination within the same job.

The current movement toward *comparable worth* policies argues that the equal pay principle should extend to work of similar difficulty, even if the jobs, themselves, are different. Because men and women are not always found doing the exact same work in the same place, and so on, the comparable worth concept argues that equal pay should apply to *equivalent* work. The problem is determining comparability. Various methods of judging the difficulty, skill, and responsibility, among other factors, required in a job have been used to judge comparability. Despite its implementation by a number of state governments and private corporations, this movement is still controversial, whereas the basic equal pay policy—equal pay for the same work—is generally accepted.

Even as women enter more lucrative fields, however—such as law, medicine, engineering, business—it is apparent that their advancement to the highest and best-paid levels of these professions has been limited. Currently, for example, women hold only about 5% of the upper management positions in America's Fortune 500 corporations (Fierman, 1990); in government, as well, their advancement to top career positions has not been nearly commensurate with their numbers (Harlan, 1991-1992). According to 1990 Bureau of the Census (1992) data, female managers and executives employed full-time earned 64% of their male counterparts' salaries. Furthermore, the gap is greater at the vice president level or above: Women's salaries at this level are only 58% of their male peers' salaries (U.S. Bureau of Labor Statistics, 1992).

No definitive single explanation of the pay gap has been proposed; suggestions include organizational barriers to advancement, career interruptions, and women's desires to combine strong commitment to both work and family roles. The existence of artificial barriers to women's advancement in organizations has been termed the *glass ceiling*. In the Civil Rights Act of 1991, a Federal Glass Ceiling Commission was created, within the U.S. Department of Labor, to do systematic research on the extent of the glass ceiling problem, its apparent causes, and potential remedial policies that might help eliminate it. (Major recommendations of this commission, prior to its expiration in 1996, are reported in Appendix B in Chapter 2.)

Basically, the commission succeeded in effectively documenting the existence of the glass ceiling and identifying the specific formal and informal barriers of which it is composed. The commission found, for example, that top managers assess male and female workers differently. Men are evaluated on perceived potential, but women are more often judged on past accomplishments (Karsten, 1994, p. 16). Furthermore, in related research, only 8% of 201 CEOs of America's largest business firms (most of whom were male) said that women "lacked the aggressiveness" to be top managers, and only 5% said women needed to be more willing to relocate to progress in their careers, thus somewhat debunking two common explanations for women's failure to reach the highest corporate levels (Fisher, 1992).

The case "Did Attorney Evans Bump Her Head on the Glass Ceiling?" deals with the judgments made about advancement or promotion of professionals—in this case, attorneys—and the complexity of these decisions. It delves into the internal operations of a law firm to examine the process for selecting full partners. Issues about both formal and informal factors that affect such decisions are relevant to the case. Students will judge whether or not the glass ceiling operated in this instance.

Issues of advancement and compensation are very clearly related to each of the other four categories of gender workplace issues represented in this text. The interaction of compensation/advancement issues with occupational segregation or stereotyping have been mentioned; in the concluding chapter attention will return to this interaction, as well as the connections among compensation/advancement issues and those of career development, and balancing work and family commitments.

 Career Development and Mentoring

An examination of career development grows logically out of the documentation of barriers to women's advancement. In attempting to break the glass ceiling, professions, work organizations, and individuals have turned to a more detailed look at the ways in which successful careers develop, the necessary ingredients of success in various professions and organizations, and gender differences in the opportunities for successful career development.

The pipeline theory, previously mentioned, assumed that as women were present in careers for the requisite number of years they would naturally progress at rates similar to those of men in the same positions and holding the same general credentials. These, after all, are the basic tenets of equal treatment, and agreement that such opportunity is important formed the societal consensus in support of the equal treatment provisions of the civil rights and equal pay policies mentioned earlier. Thirty-plus years after the passage of these policies, however, it is clear from the data previously cited that women are not progressing at rates similar to those of men, even when their basic qualifications and experience are similar (National Commission on Pay Equity, 1991).

It is now common, as a result, for individual professions and occupational groups to analyze the career paths of successful leaders within their fields. Women in both law and medicine, for example, have undertaken systematic research into the reasons for their lack of equality, in both positions attained and overall compensation, with men in their profession. Similarly, women in academia have begun to study the reasons for both their lower numbers and their small percentage of positions at the highest levels, and a wide variety of studies of women in corporate America have documented the obstacles to women seeking top positions there. This type of attention, within a variety of organizations and professions, has highlighted the importance of career planning and mentoring to the professional advancement of both men and women. However, it appears that women face some special difficulties in this regard.

First, for many years women thought of their paid work in terms of "jobs" rather than careers. The woman in a two-earner family often considered herself, and was certainly considered by others, the "second income." Jobs were often held by women for short periods of time and were accepted or abandoned according to the immediate needs of her family and the degree of flexibility offered by her husband's employment. Of course, some women were the single earners for their families, even in earlier eras, but this was the exception rather than the rule. The previously mentioned employment trends of women in recent decades have altered this picture, however. Many women are in the workforce permanently, they have higher degrees of education and experience, and they seek careers rather than jobs. Thus, they need the same career-planning and career development experiences as men.

However, many young women are still reluctant to commit to long-term career planning and have difficulty finding assistance in such planning within their professions and work organizations. Men who are in supervisory or senior positions are more likely to offer to mentor young men than young women. There are often few, if any, senior women in organizations who might be available to mentor younger women. Young women are uncomfortable asking for mentoring from older men—and the men may be unwilling to offer mentoring—because of the possible connotations that might be placed on such relationships. Thus, young women are at a disadvantage in seeking mentoring relationships, which the Glass Ceiling Commission and others have determined to be critical to professional advancement.

"Medical Mentoring" addresses these issues in the context of women developing careers in medicine. The case focuses on the recent experiences of women in medicine, and it reflects the personal views of a group of female physicians about these issues. Formal mentoring arises as an option in the case, and individuals discuss a number of mentoring models and difficulties with mentoring programs. Students will develop their own suggestions for mentoring in response to the case situation.

 ## Balancing Work and Family Responsibilities

To all observers of modern gender roles in the United States, it is clear that the nature of families and the performance of family responsibilities have undergone dramatic change at the same time that the increases in women in the workforce have occurred. A majority of women with children under the age of six years now work outside the home; in 1977, 32% of mothers with children younger than one year were in the labor force, but 52% were by 1988 (Goldin, 1990, p. 216). Furthermore, many women are now single heads of household, charged with both child rearing and earning an income. Many families with children no longer have either parent available in the household during the day, many children are cared for by non-family members or grandparents, many children are on their own after school, and so on. In addition, even within two-parent households, fathers and mothers are more apt to share family responsibilities that were once totally borne by the mothers.

These changes have prompted many workers—male and female— to support changes in the workplace such as flextime, job sharing, working from home or telecommuting, on-site child care, family and parental leave, and other family support measures. Recent studies indicate that in a more competitive employment market, some progressive employers are more than willing to provide many family services as "perks" of employment. For example, in 1990 an estimated 5,400 companies provided employer-supported child care services, an increase from 600 employers in 1982 (Karsten, 1994, p. 172). These benefits are not widespread, however: The employer-supported child care figure represents only 12% of the 44,000 U.S. employers with more than 100 employees (p. 172).

Thus, many workers must still "go it alone" when it comes to balancing the demands of their work and the needs of their families (U.S. Department of Labor, 1994). Hall (1990) has reported research indicating that, for example, 73% of mothers and 35% of fathers report "a lot of stress" in trying to mesh work and family roles, whereas 11% of the women (and none of the men) encountered "extreme" stress from this source.

Furthermore, a number of studies indicate that in a majority of families with children in which both parents work outside the home, the mothers still feel more responsibility for child care issues and provision than do fathers. Working from home, as well, introduces some complexity in the balancing of family and work responsibilities. In addition, household maintenance and errands appear to be, still, primarily the woman's responsibility in a majority of working families (Shelton, 1990). According to one estimate, the total hours all women work in the workplace and in the household increased by 5% between 1959 and 1983, whereas those for men decreased by 9% (Goldin, 1990, p. 212). This is not to discount the reality that fathers are assuming more family responsibilities; family concerns generally, however, still receive more time and physical and emotional attention from women than from men.

Government policy on these matters has focused primarily on the financial burdens of paying for child care. The Family and Medical Leave Act of 1993 represents the only national public policy addressed to other family concerns of the employed; it provides for unpaid leave for a variety of family needs and is included here as Appendix A in Chapter 4. The 1995 Welfare Reform Act continues a federal policy of providing some subsidized child care to lower-income families, and tax law revisions in the 1997 Taxpayer Relief Act extended some deductions to other families for child-related expenses. The needs of their children and, increasingly, of their elderly parents as well, continue to be a major concern of working women in all types of professions and work situations. Balancing the needs of families and the demands of work, then, continues to be an important gender-related issue in the workplace.

"The Pregnant Professor" case raises some of these issues, as they affect a dual-career couple in academia. The couple portrayed in the case takes an egalitarian approach to both family and professional issues and decisions. Issues of pregnancy leave policies, career development in the context of high employer expectations, commuting marriage arrangements, and the stress of combining professional and young family responsibilities all emerge in this case. Students view these matters through the eyes of the couple experiencing them, in the early years of their careers and marriage.

Sexual Harassment

The Anita Hill sexual harassment charges against Supreme Court nominee Clarence Thomas in 1991, as well as charges against the president and several other prominent leaders later in that decade, have focused attention on issues of sexual harassment in the workplace. The development of organizational policies and procedures for dealing with sexual harassment is now commonplace, although the effectiveness of many of these policies remains to be demonstrated.

The extent of harassment appears far more widespread than many initially believed, with close to half of American working women reporting in a variety of surveys that they have encountered some form of harassment at work. Surveys conducted in the 1970s and 1980s estimated that between 57% and 88% of employees had been harassed then (Ford & McLaughlin, 1988). A 1988-1989 study of harassment in the U.S. military revealed that two thirds of the women and 17% of the men had been harassed (Schmidt, 1990). In 1991, 53% of 1,300 members of the National Association of Female Executives reported that either they, themselves, or someone they knew had been harassed at work (Galen, Weber, & Cuneo, 1991). In 1992, 60% of the 9,000 readers who responded to a *Working Woman* survey had been sexually harassed. The first task in addressing this issue appears to be that of defining the types of harassment so that the behaviors become recognizable. Beyond that initial step, training and awareness programs are needed, it is hoped, to reduce the incidence of harassment in the workplace. Strong commitment to a policy of "no tolerance" on the part of top management also appears an essential ingredient of efforts to reduce sexual harassment.

Research suggests that most sexual harassment is committed by men against women, although the reverse is certainly possible and even same-sex harassment has been declared illegal by the U.S. Supreme Court. Women file more harassment charges than men, but the number of men reporting harassment has also increased. Harassment is also most often an issue of power, with harassers often holding organizational power or supervisory authority over those they harass. Harassment is defined as follows:

> Unwelcome sexual advances, requests for sexual favors, and other verbal or physical conduct of a sexual nature constitutes sexual harassment when submission to or rejection of this conduct explicitly or implicitly affects an individual's employment, unreasonably interferes with an individual's work performance, or creates an intimidating, hostile, or offensive work environment. (U.S. Equal Employment Opportunity Commission, 1997 [Online]. Available: http://www.eeoc.gov)

The two types of harassment are *quid pro quo* harassment, which involves the provision or denial of favorable job conditions, pay raises, or promotions based on acceptance or rejection of requests for sexual favors, and *hostile environment* sexual harassment, which occurs when verbal physical or graphic sexual displays are so pervasive that they interfere with work performance or cause an offensive or intimidating atmosphere in the workplace.

Harassment is difficult to address because it usually requires the less powerful in a work organization to confront the more powerful. It is also often the case that a general atmosphere or culture in the organization exists in support of the harassing behaviors, especially those of the "hostile environment" variety and those involving less physical behavior. As more and more young workers devote much of their time to their careers, it is also possible that many more office romances are likely to develop. Distinguishing these mutual relationships and behaviors from the unwelcome sexual harassment activity can also be a complicated exercise in some cases. Finally, the legal definitions of sexual harassment, and who is accountable for it, are in flux and being developed by the courts on a case-by-case basis. This means that many employees and organizations are understandably unclear about both what behavior is unacceptable and what organizations need to do to help reduce or eliminate it from the workplace.

"Sexual Harassment in the Army," the sexual harassment case in this collection, is based on actual incidents that occurred in the U.S. Army in the early 1990s. Revealed from the perspectives of both alleged victims of the harassment and Army leaders attempting to eliminate the harassment, the case illustrates the importance of the power relationship between harassers and their victims in perpetuating the harassment behaviors. The difficulty of creating effective protections and procedures for dealing with harassment is also clear in this case. Finally, the case documents the extent of harassment in the Army over a period of years and asks students to confront the issue of how to change an organizational culture that has tolerated harassment to this extent.

Effective Use of the Text

The book envisions an active classroom or learning environment, in which both students and teachers are committed to exploring these gender issues in an "up close and personal" fashion. From the student or trainee perspective, the best way to use the cases is to read them in advance of the group discussions and contemplate each of the questions or assignments in the Student Response section carefully. The most effective learning will occur when students are able to truly place themselves within the case and approach assignments and discussion of the issues from the perspective of those actually involved in the case situation. If so indicated by the instructor, some additional reading on topics related to the cases may also be useful in developing perspective.

From the instructor's or facilitator's point of view, it is important to fully review each case in the *Instructor's Notes*, because it provides additional resources and information that will assist in the discussion of case issues. Epilogues to each case, also presented in the *Instructor's Notes*, also reveal which course of action the actual principals in the case pursued, and what occurred as a result. Some additional teaching suggestions and techniques are also offered in the *Instructor's Notes*. Instructors should feel free, however, to adapt these suggested assignments to the particular class or training setting in which the cases are being used.

Furthermore, instructors and facilitators should try to maintain a position that there is no "right answer" to the problems or assignments posed in the cases, for, in fact, that is true. If we knew the right answer to balancing work and family, preventing sexual harassment, developing women's long-term careers, eliminating the glass ceiling, and so on, there would be no need for cases to explore the dilemmas these issues pose in the modern workplace. Rather, we could simply teach the solutions. As indicated in this discussion, however, these gender issues in the workplace are more complex and varied than a single solution or approach acknowledges. Furthermore, practitioners in a wide variety of organizations and scholars are very much in the process of exploring alternative ways of addressing these problems. The cases' value, then, lies in the validity and complexity of the issues they pose and their power to engage students and instructors alike in exploring possible effective actions addressed to these issues. A particular student's response, then, *if well reasoned and based on the facts at hand*, is just as likely to have merit as anyone else's. If instructors have difficulty in maintaining that view and openness, they probably should not be teaching these issues with the case method.

Suggested Readings

Cockburn, C. (1991). *In the way of women: Men's resistance to sex equality in organizations.* Ithaca: Cornell University, New York State School of Industrial and Labor Relations.

Epstein, C. F. (1993). *Women in law.* Urbana and Chicago: University of Illinois Press.

Pregnancy Discrimination Act of 1978, 42 U.S.C. at 2000e (k).

Ries, P., & Stone, A. J. (Eds.). (1993). *The American woman, 1992-93: A status report.* New York: Norton.

Sandroff, R. (1992, June). Sexual harassment: The inside story. *Working Woman,* pp. 47-51.

Stoner, C., & Hartman, R. (1990, May/June). Family responsibilities and career progress: The good, the bad, and the ugly. *Business Horizons,* pp. 7-14.

Wood, R. G., Corcoran, M. E., & Courant, P. N. (1993, July). Pay differences among the highly paid: The male-female earnings gap in lawyers' salaries. *Journal of Labor Economics, 11,* 417-440.

 References

Civil Rights Act of 1964, Title VII, 42 U.S.C. at 2000e et seq.

Civil Rights Act of 1991, P.L. 102-166.

Fierman, J. (1990, July 30). Why women still don't hit the top. *Fortune,* pp. 40-66.

Fisher, A. (1992, September 21). When will women get to the top? *Fortune,* pp. 44-56.

Ford, R., & McLaughlin, F. (1988). Sexual harassment at work. *Business Horizons, 31*(6), 14-19.

Galen, M., Weber, J., & Cuneo, A. (1991, October 18). Sexual harassment: Out of the shadows. *Business Week,* pp. 31-31.

Goldin, C. (1990). *Understanding the gender gap: An economic history of American women.* Oxford, UK: Oxford University Press.

Hall, D. (1990, Winter). Balancing work life and home life: What can organizations do to help? *Academy of Management Executive, 2,* 213-223.

Harlan, S. (1991-1992, Winter). Women face barriers in top management. *Women in Public Services: A Bulletin for the Center for Women in Government, 2.*

Jencks, C., Perman, L., & Rainwater, L. (1988). What is a good job? A new measure of labor-market success. *American Journal of Sociology, 93,* 1322-1357.

Karsten, M. F. (1994). *Management and gender: Issues and attitudes.* Westport, CT: Praeger.

National Commission on Pay Equity. (1991). After 28 years, equal pay for equal work still not achieved. *Newsnotes, 12*(1), 3.

Reskin, B., & Padavic, I. (1994). *Women and men at work.* Thousand Oaks, CA: Pine Forge Press.

Schmidt, E. (1990, September 12). Two in three military women report harassment. *Wisconsin State Journal,* p. 2A.

Shelton, B. (1990). The distribution of household tasks: Does wife's employment status make a difference? *Journal of Family Issues, 11,* 115-135.

U.S. Bureau of the Census. (1992). *Detailed occupation and other characteristics from the EEO file for the United States* (1990 Census of Population supplementary reports, 1990 CP-S-1-1). Washington, DC: Government Printing Office.

U.S. Bureau of Labor Statistics. (1992, January). *Employment and earnings 39.* Washington, DC: U.S. Department of Labor.

U.S. Department of Labor. (1994). *Working wives count!* Washington, DC: Government Printing Office.

U.S. Equal Employment Opportunity Commission [Online]. (1997). Available: http://www.eeoc.gov.

CASE STUDIES

CHAPTER 1

Half a Pie, or None?

CASE OVERVIEW *This case involves potential sexual discrimination in the form of sexual stereotyping of work. Important issues applying to organizational culture and individual career development apply to the situations in the case. Students must evaluate a corporate structure and culture from the viewpoint of a real job applicant, first, and then from the viewpoints of both this woman as an employee and one of her supervisors. Three different "decision points" occur in the case, and students are asked to respond at each of these points.*

 Body of Case

"Are you prepared to accept our offer of the position of project manager, Ms. Andersen?" asked Mr. Green, president of Computer Central.

Ms. Andersen recalled her hours of consideration of this reduced offer, which she had suspected would be forthcoming, in contrast to the position for which she had actively applied. To accept "half a pie" or not posed the first of many dilemmas she would face regarding Computer Central and the next stage of her career.

Background

Kirsten Andersen was by 1994 a highly qualified senior management consultant and business developer. She had extensive background,

training, and experience in the area of market and business development. Holding a B.A. in economics and international marketing, M.A.
degrees in international communication and international law and organization, and a finance certificate from the Wharton School of Business, she had also completed all the course work for a doctorate in
political sociology.

In the early 1990s, Ms. Andersen built a successful consulting
firm that helped develop 15 Fortune 200 companies in the areas of research, design, and implementation of foreign market entry strategies,
and integration of technical systems. In 1994, Ms. Andersen sold her
firm for over $1 million, and pondered her next career move. Her goals
were to acquire more technical consulting and business development
experience abroad and to work within a major corporate structure, to
enhance her marketability for senior executive positions. She also
wanted an opportunity to aggressively pursue the high earnings she
had attained in her own firm.

The Half-a-Pie Offer

Early in her job search, a colleague provided entry to Computer
Central, a European firm developing new technical enterprises in the
emerging democracies of eastern Europe, and part of the worldwide
umbrella corporation, Techniques Advantage. Computer Central re-
tained its most qualified personnel in the position of evaluator, which
involved assessment of new projects and presentation of recommendations to clients about technical strategy. The position also carried
with it substantial sale and bonus income potential. Attaining an
evaluator's slot, then, would have met all of Ms. Andersen's career
objectives in 1994.

Ms. Andersen was interviewed for the evaluator's position at
Computer Central in January 1995. She met with Mr. Jones, vice president
of Computer Central, as well as with Mr. Green, the firm's president.
She was also interviewed by CEO Charles, worldwide head of Techniques Advantage. Each of these individuals told her in interviews
that she was well qualified to be an evaluator; Mr. Green, in particular,
told her that "you will be an asset to our evaluators' team." Mr. Green

also told Ms. Andersen that Mr. Jones said, "She definitely is an evaluator."

In late January 1995, Mr. Green submitted Ms. Andersen's name for final approval for appointment as an evaluator. Shortly thereafter, however, he reported to Ms. Andersen that CEO Charles of Techniques Advantage stated she could not be hired as an evaluator because "no woman will be on my evaluators' team." Mr. Charles had privately elaborated his opinion that the energy, drive, and commitment required of evaluators was beyond what most women could offer a firm.

Mr. Green then attempted to persuade Ms. Andersen to come to work for Computer Central under a different job title. He assured her informally that she would be given evaluator duties and eventually converted to the proper job title, once she was working on projects in Europe. As incentive, Mr. Green agreed to pay a base salary commensurate with that of beginning evaluators and to provide her with per diem payment, at the evaluator rather than at the standard operations rate. (However, Ms. Andersen would initially have no sales and limited bonus income possibilities.) Mr. Green fully intended to help Ms. Andersen move into an evaluator's position at the earliest moment acceptable to the corporation and was confident that this would occur.

(See Student Response section for Decision Point 1 alternatives for Ms. Andersen and Mr. Green.)

Half a Pie Remains Half

Based on these conditions, and assuming that she would be assigned evaluation duties as well as quickly converted to evaluator status, Ms. Andersen accepted Computer Central's offer, and was hired in February 1995 as a project manager.

With her extensive technical background, Ms. Andersen was soon in great demand for work on the evaluators' teams, under the supervision of various senior evaluators. From February through December 1995, she worked on projects in Europe. Although she worked on evaluation teams, she was nonetheless designated a project manager. She was not allowed to make presentations of the technical findings to clients; instead, she was required to write scripts for the senior evaluators' presentations, even in cases for which they lacked the technical expertise to present or explain the information fully. Lacking the official title of evaluator, Ms. Andersen was also not given a team to oversee.

At the end of the year, Ms. Andersen spoke with the head of the European evaluation team, asking for the chance to move into an evaluator's slot. This individual told her that she had to "carry the bags" to "earn her wings"—something she felt she had been doing the previous six months, and that, to her knowledge, other (male) evaluators had not been required to do. The head of the European team also proposed that she work on an evaluation for a major client who had wanted a technical, rather than a productivity, evaluation, and told her, "This is your shot." At about this time, Ms. Andersen learned from two other female project managers that they, also, had been hired with expectations of moving into evaluator positions.

Ms. Andersen gladly accepted her newest assignment. She soon discovered, however, that a senior and a junior evaluator, neither of whom had any particular technical background, were also assigned to this new technical evaluation. She worked hard on the project and developed the presentation of the technical aspects the client had requested. She was then excluded from the final two meetings with the client, when the sale was to have taken place. The sale was not made, and Ms. Andersen later was told that she had "blown her chance" to become an evaluator. She reported these developments informally to Mr. Green, who had initially hired her; he continued to believe that an evaluator's position was "just around the corner" for Ms. Andersen.

(See Student Response section for Decision Point 2 alternatives for Ms. Andersen and Mr. Green.)

Pie in the Face

In fall 1996, Computer Central merged with another subsidiary of Techniques Advantage, as part of a general reorganization. At this time, the head of the new European Evaluation unit asked for a list of ten employees to be converted to evaluators, since technical knowledge was needed for the expanded evaluation team. Because Ms. Andersen was the only employee already working (in other than an evaluator's position) on evaluation teams in Europe, it was widely assumed that she would be selected as one of the ten new evaluators. However, the executive selected ten men and immediately promoted them to evaluator positions. Of the two European selectees, one was a programmer, and the other a project manager in operations who had repeatedly stated that he had no interest in the high-stress position of evaluator.

Shortly thereafter, in October 1996, Ms. Andersen, at her own request, met with the president of the newly merged firm. She informed him that she had been hired to perform evaluator's duties and wanted to be appointed to that position. The president acknowledged that there was a "different culture" within Techniques Advantage that needed to be changed and that "he needed strong people like her to help him." He proposed that Ms. Andersen complete an operations installment in the short run, and he promised that he would confirm with the head of European Evaluation that she would then join the evaluation team as an evaluator. The president informed her later that day that the evaluation team head had said he would be "delighted to have her on his evaluation team, after a little more experience."

Once again, Ms. Andersen agreed. As part of the new arrangement, she was asked to substitute a three-week home leave rotation for the standard six-week length rotation. To accommodate the company, she agreed to the suggested reduction in home rotation, as well.

Ms. Andersen work effectively on the operations project; in fact, her work set the standard for the other employees, with regard to the presentation of analytical material, as well as for structural reorganization and staffing recommendations.

Soon after joining the project, however, she began receiving a series of inaccurate, unusual, and unwarranted memos from Mr. Lawton, head of operations. These memos dealt with minor matters related to her work schedule, such a being an hour late for arrival, even though she and her co-workers did not punch time clocks and routinely worked nights and weekends. In particular, Mr. Lawson criticized her use of her home-leave rotation, even though the three-week rather than six-week cycle was undertaken at the request of the company.

Ms. Andersen was sufficiently disturbed by these actions that in March 1996 she wrote to Mr. Green, and subsequently met with him to discuss her concerns and what action she should pursue next. She was particularly upset about the loss of opportunity and earnings, due to being passed over for the evaluators' openings, and the recent unwarranted memos. Clearly, some additional action on her part was warranted, but she was uncertain as to what course to pursue next.

(See Student Response section for Decision Point 3 alternatives for Ms. Andersen and Mr. Green.)

Suggested Readings

Karsten, M. F. (1994). *Management and gender: Issues and attitudes.* Westport, CT: Praeger.

Konek, C. W., & Kitch, S. L. (1994). *Women and careers.* Thousand Oaks, CA: Sage.

Mandell, B., & Kohler-Gray, S. (1990). Management development that values diversity. *Personnel,* pp. 41-47.

Reskin, B., & Padavic, I. (1994). *Women and men at work.* Thousand Oaks, CA: Pine Forge Press.

Twomey, D. (1990). *Equal employment opportunity law.* Chicago: South-Western.

Wind, A. (1995). [Demand letter for client]. Washington, DC: Wind & Associates.

Student Response

Decision Point 1: The Job Offer

1. Assume the role of Mr. Green, who has been told that "women don't throw themselves into their work enough" to be evaluators. Why doesn't Mr. Green confront his superior, CEO Charles, with the issue of sexual stereotyping of the evaluator's position? If you choose to confront the issue at this point, how might you do so?

2. Assume the role of the job applicant, Ms. Andersen. Should Ms. Andersen accept this lower-level position, even though executives of Computer Central seem to agree she is qualified for the evaluator's job for which she has applied?

Decision Point 2:
Initial Experience in the Firm

1. Assume the role of Ms. Andersen. After encountering sexual stereotypes of the type of work and presentations you are allowed to engage in, as well as similar treatment of several other women, what major action alternatives can you identify? Which of these do you prefer, and why?

2. Assume the role of Mr. Green. Ms. Andersen has spoken to you about her frustrations with sexual stereotyping in relation to her assignments, and similar experiences of several other women. How might you affect the climate of the organization on these matters?

Decision Point 3: After Evaluators' Positions Are
Awarded to Men

1. Assume the role of Ms. Andersen. Should you continue your responsibilities hoping for an evaluator's position later, resign, pursue legal action, or some combination of these options?

2. What evidence of sex discrimination is there in this case?

3. Assume the role of Mr. Green. Identify your alternatives. Should Ms. Andersen pursue legal remedies? Which of these alternatives do you prefer, and why?

APPENDIX A

Title VII of the
Civil Rights Act of 1964

The following sections are taken directly from Title VII of the Civil Rights Act of 1964 (Public Law 88-352) as it appears in Volume 42 of the United States Code, beginning at Section 2000e. Title VII prohibits employment discrimination based on race, color, religion, sex, or national origin.

Under this law, companies employing 15 or more people are prevented from discriminating in the areas of

- Hiring and firing

- Compensation and promotion

- Transfer or layoff

- Job advertisement and recruitment

- Testing

- Training and apprenticeship programs

- Use of company facilities

- Fringe benefits, retirement plans, and disability leave

The Civil Rights Act of 1991 (Public Law 102-166) amends several sections of Title VII related to the proving of the "disparate impact" of employer's actions on different groups of employees, and the awarding of damages in such cases. The Equal Pay Act is another amendment to Title VII; it requires that an employer pay all employees equally for equal work, regardless of gender. The law covers situations where men and women perform jobs that require equal skill, effort, and responsibility. The exception to this law is a pay system that is based on a factor other than gender, such as seniority, or the quantity or quality of items produced or processed.

An employer is expected to post notices describing the federal laws prohibiting job discrimination based on race, color, sex, national origin, religion, age, or disability, and describing the provisions of the Equal Pay Act. The Equal Employment Opportunity Commission (EEOC) was created in the 1964 Civil Rights Act to investigate and, if necessary, prosecute in court violations of the employment provisions of the law. The EEOC publishes clear guidelines on how to file complaints of employment discrimination.

Unlawful Employment Practices (Title VII, 1964 Civil Rights Act)

Sec. 2000e-2. (Section 703)

(a) It shall be an unlawful employment practice for an employer—

    (1) to fail or refuse to hire or to discharge any individual, or otherwise to discriminate against any individual with respect to his compensation, terms, conditions, or privileges of employment, because of such individual's race, color, religion, sex, or national origin; or

    (2) to limit, segregate, or classify his employees or applicants for employment in any way which would deprive or tend to deprive any individual of employment opportunities or otherwise adversely affect his status as an employee, because of such individual's race, color, religion, sex, or national origin.

(b) It shall be an unlawful employment practice for an employment agency to fail or refuse to refer for employment, or otherwise to discriminate against, any individual because of his race, color, religion, sex, or national origin, or to classify or refer for employment any individual on the basis of his race, color, religion, sex, or national origin.

(c) It shall be an unlawful employment practice for any employer, labor organization, or joint labor-management committee controlling apprenticeship or other training or retraining, including on-the-job training programs, to discriminate against any individual because of his race, color, religion, sex, or national origin in admission to, or employment in, any program established to provide apprenticeship or other training.

CHAPTER 2

Did Attorney Evans Bump Her Head on the Glass Ceiling?

CASE OVERVIEW *This case describes the denial of a partner-ship to a seemingly well-qualified female attorney in a pres-tigious law firm. The decision-making process used by the firm is documented, as well as subsequent court decisions contesting the firm's action. Issues related to gender dis-crimination in professional advancement, particularly the glass ceiling phenomenon, are the focus of the case. In de-scribing the results of legal action following the firm's deci-sion, the case also points out the difficulties of proving that discrimination has occurred, in a decision that involves con-siderable employer latitude.*

Body of Case

Meghan Evans sat stunned in her attorney's office. Word had just been received that a federal appeals court had reversed a district court de-cision, in which Ms. Evans had initially won her lawsuit against her former employers, based on her claims of glass ceiling discrimination. The appeals court, however, reversed the lower court, ruling that her employers—a major law firm—had not been guilty of glass ceiling dis-crimination. The decision she now faced was, should she appeal this latest decision to the U.S. Supreme Court?

"I simply cannot *believe* this new ruling," Meghan exploded. "The firm is so clearly discriminating against women! Is there nothing else we can do?"

"Frankly, Meghan, your judgment as an attorney is nearly as experienced as mine," stated Meghan's attorney. "There are obviously two different interpretations represented by the district court and the appeals court decisions, and we have to decide whether our case seems strong enough to prevail at the Supreme Court level. Of course you know *I* believe totally in the correctness of our position, but the decision will have to be yours."

Across town, in the law offices of Wilson, Barnes, Sauer, and Kahn, the scene was quite different. "I knew we'd win on appeal," exulted partner Barnes. "She simply didn't have enough evidence of sex discrimination when the entire process was reviewed."

"I wonder if she'll appeal to the Supreme Court," responded another partner in the firm. "It's not so clear whether our position on the discrimination issues, or hers, would prevail at that level."

"I certainly hope this is the end of it," said Barnes.

Background

Meghan Evans managed, despite the added responsibilities of raising two children on her own, to complete law school with an outstanding record. Widely recruited by prestigious firms in the late 1980s, and highly ambitious, she settled on Wilson, Barnes, Sauer, and Kahn, a firm of over 200 attorneys. Her goal was to be a successful trial attorney, and she served in the litigation department of Wilson, Barnes. After six years, Ms. Evans's superiors in the litigation department, with whom she had worked most closely, wanted her to be named a partner in the firm.

The Firm's Evaluation

The evaluation process to become a full partner at Wilson, Barnes, as in many large firms, was complex. It relied on personal networking and respect of existing partners—often heavily influenced by the visibility and importance of the cases to which the associate had been assigned—as well as an assessment of a portfolio of hundreds of written evaluations for the associate.

In these portfolio evaluations, those working with the attorney in question scored her in 20 different specific categories, and also gave her an overall performance rating or score. Associates within two years of partnership consideration were reviewed annually; nonsenior associates were evaluated semiannually.

The firm's partners submitted the written evaluations on standardized forms. The partner described the degree of contact with the associate during the evaluation period, but evaluations were required regardless of the extent of the evaluating partner's contact with the associate's work. The process attempted to recognize that successful attorneys need to be evaluated in a wide variety of areas, using a composite picture of their talents, rather than a single attribute or skill.

For this reason, ten criteria of legal performance were listed on the forms: legal analysis, legal writing and drafting, research skills, formal speech, informal speech, judgment, creativity, negotiating and advocacy, promptness, and efficiency. Ten personal characteristics were also included: reliability, taking and managing responsibility, flexibility, growth potential, attitude, client relationship, client servicing and development, ability under pressure, ability to work independently, and dedication.

Partners provided "grades" as well as written comments on these criteria. The evaluation forms described the grades as follows:

1. *Distinguished:* Outstanding, exceptional; consistently demonstrates extraordinary adeptness and quality; star.

2. *Good:* Displays particular merit on a consistent basis; effective work product and performance; able; talented.

3. *Acceptable:* Satisfactory; adequate; displays neither particular merit nor any serious defects or omissions; dependable.

4. *Marginal:* Inconsistent work product and performance; *sometimes* below the level of what you expect from associates.

5. *Unacceptable:* Fails to meet minimum standard of quality expected of an associate at this level; *frequently* below the acceptable level.

Evaluating partners were also asked to describe any particular strengths or weaknesses of an associate. In addition, partners were told to indicate their views on the admission of each senior associate to the partnership from among these five choices: "with enthusiasm," "with favor," "with mixed emotions," "with negative feelings," or "no opinion." Finally, partners were asked to respond yes or no to the following general question: "I would feel comfortable turning over to this associate to handle on his/her own a significant matter for one of my clients."

In addition to recommendations of partners and the evaluation of portfolios, the review process included some quantitative measures of performance, such as hours billed, business generated, new business attracted to the firm, and so on. The review of the associate's record, including the evaluations submitted by all partners who cared to do so, was initially conducted by a ten-partner Associates Committee; upon their favorable partnership recommendation, the matter was reviewed by a five-member Executive Committee, which makes recommendations to the entire group of partners, numbering 94 at the time of Ms. Evans's consideration. However, only those associates nominated by the Executive Committee would be voted on by the entire partnership.

Meghan anticipated that her partnership seemed almost a foregone conclusion at Wilson, Barnes. Her superiors in the litigation department wanted her as a partner. They admired and respected her work, and they liked her as a person. In addition, in respect to the portfolio evaluation system, Meghan's reviews from the partners for whom she had done substantial work were consistently positive for the entire six years of her service. Even though such matters are obviously subjective and difficult to measure, she believed that a majority of the partners in the firm clearly seemed to respond favorably to her, both personally and professionally.

Despite this seemingly rosy picture, the ten-partner Associates Committee in 1988 recommended, by a vote of nine to one, against Meghan Evans's promotion to full partner. They did, however, recommend to the Executive Committee that she be offered a special partnership in the domestic relations department of the firm, a unit from which two partners were leaving the firm, and where they believed her skills would be most useful. The Associates Committee suggested that she might be able to make full partnership relatively soon in this department, because of her positive evaluations on work with clients and in the courtroom. The Executive Committee did a special review of the material on Ms. Evans as well as one of the negative recommendations against her partnership. It concluded that she should not be offered full partnership and stated the reason was her lack of legal analysis ability.

The field of domestic relations has often been one of the most available specialties for women attorneys; Meghan believed she was being told that she must practice in the "women's part" of the firm. Furthermore, given the nature of modern marriages, this work presents complex legal issues. The analytical skills required are daunting, especially with regard to the taxation issues involved. Thus, Ms. Evans, with six years of experience in business litigation, believed that she lacked the requisite background for the domestic relations work.

Believing that she was being denied full partnership on the basis of sex discrimination, Meghan resigned and initiated her lawsuit against Wilson, Barnes.

The Initial Court Decision

Meghan Evans and her labor attorney agreed that her denial of partnership constituted discrimination on the basis of sex. Meghan recalled many indications of such possible discrimination. "In my initial job interview with the firm," she remembered, "a partner told me it would not be easy for me at Wilson because 'I was a woman, had not attended an Ivy League law school, and had not been on law review.' " Meghan also felt, at times, that she was given less desirable assignments, with less visibility, than her male counterparts received. This, of course, would affect her impressions on attorneys with whom she worked less closely.

"Meghan also could provide specific crude and unprofessional statements made by one of the firm's male attorneys to female attorneys," recalled her lawyer, "which demonstrate a work environment hostile to women."

"I think we can prove discrimination, here," said her attorney in their initial meeting. "We will need to prove that the reason given for your denial—lack of sufficient legal analysis ability—was really a 'cover,' or pretext, for gender discrimination. We also need to point out the instances in which your male colleagues were treated differently than you were in the evaluation process. Since the evaluation is essentially a subjective one, we should be able to show how influenced it might be by gender bias. Further, there are only ten women partners in the firm, which strengthens our claim."

Meghan reviewed some of the additional evidence of discrimination. The senior partner who chaired the Executive Committee later stated that he rated Ms. Evans low on "client satisfaction," despite high ratings in this area in her portfolio. The chair provided no specific facts in support of his rating, stating only that his opinion was that she was a prima donna. She was criticized by another senior partner for weak legal analysis skills, yet her overall rating in this area was the same as some of the male associates with whom she had been compared. In the Associates Committee's review, Ms. Evans was also criticized for being "too involved with women's issues in the firm," and "very demanding" and "insufficiently 'nonassertive and acquiescent' to the predominantly male partnership." These comments suggested that she might have been punished in her review for raising issues in the firm or for not conforming to a submissive image or style.

At the time the Executive Committee at Wilson, Barnes declined to recommend Ms. Evans for partner, Meghan and her attorney maintained, it did see fit to recommend a number of other associates. Out of a total of eight candidates in her class, five male associates and one female associate were recommended for regular partnership. One male associate was not recommended for either regular or special partnership. The evaluation portfolio data on the male associates indicated that a few received higher ratings than Ms. Evans. The majority of the men recommended for partner were not superior to her, however, according to the district court's analysis. The quantitative measures of associate success—including total hours billed, volume of business generated, and clients individually attracted to the firm— presented a picture of Ms. Evans's performance as equal to most of the men and superior to some who were recommended for partner. In addition, Ms. Evans had actually tried several cases, which was unusual for an associate in litigation, because many cases are settled without trial, and the few tried are usually handled by partners. The volume of business generated by Ms. Evans had steadily increased in the several years just prior to her review for partner, and her colleagues in the litigation department remarked on this as an indicator of her likely future productivity for the firm.

Meghan's case also stressed the argument that several male associates were made partner despite scathing reviews in their portfolios; the cited failings of these associates were not used to block their recommendation for partnerships. A number were made partners despite serious concerns about general competence and behavior. One male associate was even deemed by the partners to have committed malpractice, and yet was recommended for partner by the Executive Committee. The committee went so far as to excuse another male associate's frequent, lengthy, and unexplained absences (which created potential liability for the firm due to missed deadlines), because of his abilities in another area. Ms. Evans maintained that these recommendations were in stark contrast with her own evaluation, in which criticism of her analytical abilities—about which partners disagreed, and for which her overall rating in 1988 was more than satisfactory—was given so much emphasis in the final evaluation. She believed that this criticism was unfairly used to negate her entire track record of accomplishment in the firm in other areas of the evaluation. Indeed, Evans was convinced she had met and in many ways exceeded the explicit standards the firm had set and that she evidenced none of the serious character flaws manifested by more than one male associate accepted for partner.

This, then, was the basis of Meghan's original lawsuit. She claimed both that the firm's stated reason for her denial of partnership—lack of legal analysis skill—was a pretext for gender discrimination and that she had been treated differently than male colleagues. Written reviews of men who had made partner the same year Ms. Evans was denied were read into the testimony in the case. (Some of these were so embarrassing to the firm—one man had committed malpractice and another had disappeared without notice and missed critical deadlines—that Wilson, Barnes later had the names of these individuals removed from the record.)

"It is a classic glass ceiling case," her attorney argued, "denying a woman advancement to the highest levels of the professions and management on the basis of sex, while making up other excuses." The judge in the initial district court trial agreed, and found in favor of Evans, citing over 160 findings of fact in support of her contention of discrimination on the basis of sex.

The Appellate Court Reverses

The firm of Wilson, Barnes, however, appealed the initial decision, and the three judges on the Circuit Court of Appeals overturned the initial verdict. In their opinion, there were several compelling arguments that Evans failed to prove sex discrimination.

First, the appeals court believed that the district court had been very selective in its review of the evaluation data on Meghan Evans and her male associates who did receive partnerships. The appeals court, for example, argued that the evaluations of Ms. Evans's legal analytical ability had been quite critical, beginning in her early years with the firm, and continuing in her final Associates Committee reviews, in 1987 and 1988 (see Appendix A). The appeals court concluded that there was substantial evidence that Ms. Evans did not meet the firm's standards for legal analysis.

To the argument that Ms. Evans's other positive evaluations should have been allowed to offset some limitations in legal analysis, the appeals court responded that the judgment of the firm should prevail on this matter. Their basic reasoning was that courts owe partnerships "special deference" in their employment decisions. This line of argument stems from the presumption that small business associations ought not to be dictated to by law, but retain much latitude of judgment about selecting members and partners who fit the organization. This is an application of "freedom of association" to small firms and groups.

Furthermore, the appellate court argued that it is not the job of the court to substitute its judgment about employment for that of the employer himself. The appellate judges asserted that the district court, in its initial ruling, had substituted *its own* judgment about employment decisions and qualifications for that of the law firm's Associates and Executive Committees and that this substitution of judgment on the part of the district court was improper. The appellate decision stated that the proper analysis should not have been whether in the court's view the lack of legal analytical ability was crucial to success as a partner. Rather, the court should have analyzed whether male associates who were granted partnership had been similarly criticized. The opinion of the appeals court stated that "the district court's comparison of plaintiff with successful male candidates in categories *other than* legal analytic ability did not lend support to that court's finding of pretext, and district court ignored evidence the firm produced to compare plaintiff's shortcomings with strengths of successful male candidates *within* the category of legal analytic ability."

The appeals court also decided that the evidence of a "hostile" environment toward women at Wilson, Barnes was not convincing. It stated that the attorney who had made "offensive" remarks to women had left the firm before Ms. Evans's partnership decision was made, that he had been reprimanded, and that he was unlikely to make partner in any event. The court also stated that the firm's having a small number of women partners did not, in itself, prove discrimination against women. Finally, the appellate decision also concluded that evidence of discrimination in the assignments Ms. Evans was given was not sufficient to prove such discrimination on the basis of sex.

The appeals court thus found that the firm's judgment was permissible, because it had the right to determine its own qualifications for partnership. It also determined that evidence of discrimination on the basis of sex was not sufficient in this situation to establish that the stated reason for the firm's decision was a pretext to cover discrimination.

Is This Over?

Opponents of the appellate court decision urged Meghan Evans to petition the U.S. Supreme Court to review the case. Yale Law Professor Benson called the appeals decision "a hideous miscarriage of justice," and many other Evans supporters claimed that the courts should prevent private firms such as Wilson, Barnes from using their freedom to exercise business judgment as a cover for prejudice and unlawful, unconstitutional discrimination in their employment practices. Seeing the Evans case as symbolic of the glass ceiling operating against the promotion of women and minorities to the highest and most lucrative positions in U.S. professions and businesses, over 60 groups offered to file amicus curiae ("friend of the court") briefs in support of Ms. Evans's Supreme Court petition. Women's and civil rights groups, in particular, shared Ms. Evans's outrage over the appeals court ruling.

On the basis of the information presented here, do you agree with the initial court's ruling, in favor of Ms. Evans, or with the reversal in the appeals court? Why?

Should Meghan appeal this decision to the U.S. Supreme Court?

 Suggested Readings

Epstein, C. F., with Saute, R., Oglensky, B., & Gever, M. (1995). Glass ceilings and open doors: Women's advancement in the legal profession: A report to the Committee on Women in the Profession, The Association of the Bar of the City of New York [Summary]. *Fordham Law Review, 64,* 302-305.

Ezold v. Wolf, Block, Schorr and Solis-Cohen, 983 F.2d 509 (3rd Cir. 1992).

Glass Ceiling Commission. (1995). *A solid investment: Making full use of the nation's human capital.* Washington, DC: Government Printing Office.

Fierman, J. (1990, July 30). Why women still don't hit the top. *Fortune,* pp. 40-62.

Jones, R. W. (1995, March 29). *About glass ceiling current cases* [Online]. Available: http://www.afrinet.net/7Ehallh/afrotalk/afromar95/0075.html.

Karsten, M. F. (1994). Equal employment. In M. F. Karsten, *Management and gender: Issues and attitudes* (pp. 39-56). Westport, CT: Praeger.

National Association of Women Lawyers. (1996, February 2). *The shoemaker's children—Employment law issues relating to women and families in the law firm: A dialogue reflecting the firm's perspective and the lawyer's perspective.* NAWL program at the American Bar Association midwinter meeting, Baltimore, MD.

Student Response

1. What is the glass ceiling? How might it be relevant to Ms. Evans's case? Review the material in Appendix B on the glass ceiling.

2. What suggestions are there in the case that *informal norms* at Wilson, Barnes might have hurt Ms. Evans's case for partnership?

3. Why would Ms. Evans bother to sue Wilson, Barnes?

4. Why did the appeals court reverse the lower court's decision in favor of Ms. Evans?

5. What is the cost to the firm of Wilson, Barnes for pursuing this case?

6. How might opportunities for women and minorities be improved in professional situations such as that described in this case?

7. Role plays or essay: Assume you are the following individual and describe (or act out) what actions you would take in the incident described in the case.

    Meghan Evans after the appeals court decision

    Ms. Evans's supervising partner, a supporter of her partnership

    The employment attorney consulted by Ms. Evans when she first learned of her denial of partnership

    A member of the Executive Committee who supported Ms. Evans's partnership

    A female senior partner, not on the Executive Committee, who supported Evans

    A young female attorney entering Wilson, Barnes as a new associate

    A female attorney two years away from a partnership decision in Wilson, Barnes

    The chair of the Executive Committee after the appeals court decision

8. Debate: Simulate a meeting of the Executive Committee in Wilson, Barnes, in which the arguments for and against granting partnership are debated. Or simulate a Supreme Court conference, in

which the justices are debating whether they should review the appeals court decision against Ms. Evans.

9. Change agent: Develop a list of recommendations to the partners of Wilson, Barnes for improving the opportunity structure for women in the firm.

Develop a list of recommendations for improving the firm's evaluation process.

APPENDIX A

Summary of Meghan Evans's Evaluations on Legal Analysis

1987 Evaluations

Partner Name	Grade (Legal Analysis)	Comments
Promin	M	"I had minimal contact with Meghan, but I thought she did not generate ideas . . . or pull the facts together well and exercise the best lawyerly judgment. She seemed somewhat in over her head, but I don't think she should have been." Recommended partnership "with negative feelings."
Kurt	A	"There seems to be serious question as to whether she has the legal ability to take on large matters and handle them on her own. We have been over this many times and there is nothing I can add to what I have already said about Meghan. What I envisioned about her when I hired her as a 'good, stand-up effective courtroom lawyer' remains true and I think she has proven her case. Apparently she has not proved to the satisfaction of the firm the other qualities considered necessary to rise to the top of the firm." Recommended partnership "with mixed emotions."
Alder	A	Slight contact. Recommended partnership "with mixed emotions."
Booke	A	"Meghan has avoided demonstrating ability in the area [of legal analysis] because I believe she lacks it. On the other hand, in her case, other qualities redeem her. . . . I would not want her in charge of a large legally complex case, the traditional measure of a Wilson, Barnes partner." Recommended partnership "with favor."

(continues)

1987 Evaluations (continued)

Partner Name	Grade (Legal Analysis)	Comments
Flahan	A	Slight contact. Recommended partnership "with mixed emotions."
Jones	M	"I have been singularly unimpressed with the level of her ability. . . . She may be fine to keep for certain smaller matters, but I don't see her skills as being those for our sophisticated practice. Recommended partnership "with negative feelings."
Smith	G	"She is excellent in court and loves to be in that arena. . . . She remains a little weak in her initial analysis of complex legal issues."
Dubrin	A	"In my one experience we lost a client, but I think Meghan performed satisfactorily." No opinion as to partnership admission.
Robins	G	Slight contact. Recommended partnership "with favor."
Spinaker	G	"Little contact, most favorable impression." Recommended partnership "with favor."
Rosen	A	"On a very complicated matter primarily involving financial analysis, I am not sure whether or not [she] grasped analysis fully. (I am not sure that others working on project did, either.)" Recommended partnership "with mixed emotions."
Tomas	A	Slight contact. Recommended partnership "with mixed emotions."
Davins	A	"She will never be a legal scholar—but we have plenty of support in that area." Recommended partnership "with enthusiasm."
Arbit	A	"Barely adequate legal skills. Her abilities are limited. She makes a good impression but she lacks real legal analytical ability." Recommended partnership "with mixed emotions."

1987 Evaluations (continued)

Partner Name	Grade (Legal Analysis)	Comments
Fiedler	M	"Meghan has certain strengths. . . . If directed, she will do a good job—except that she has limitations with respect to complex legal issues. However, when left on her own she does not do what has to be done until [the] case is in crisis and she does a poor job in keeping [the] client informed." Recommended partnership "with negative feelings."
Goldberg	M	"Would feel comfortable turning over a significant matter for one of my clients if not too complex." "Meghan reputedly can handle many of our matters on her own. If so and reliable others bear these rumors out, partnership may be in the cards." Recommended partnership "with negative feelings."
Jones	M	"Her abilities to grasp legal issues from the little I observed was insufficient to trust her in major litigation on her own." Recommended partnership "with negative feelings."
Pole	G	Slight contact. Recommended partnership "with favor."
Simmons	M	"Probably ancient history—but I do recall my perception that she does not write well and lacks intellectual sophistication." Recommended partnership "with negative feelings."
Fallows	G	"Meghan handled a moderate sized lawsuit for a client of mine. Job was done well and responsibly. Result was good."
Robins	G	Slight contact. Recommended partnership "with mixed emotions."
Gerb	M	"Experience with her years ago was unsatisfactory." No opinion on partnership.
Berman	G	Slight contact. Recommended partnership "with enthusiasm."

This summary, drawn from the appellate court records, focuses only on Meghan's grades in legal analysis, because that was the firm's reason for denial of her partnership.

The district court omitted from its findings the following statements on Evans's legal analytical ability: Booke's, Kurt's, and Smith's.

The above is a summary of the Associates Committee's evaluation in this area, and does not include all comments.

In 1988, 91 partners submitted evaluations of Evans. Thirty-two, slightly over one third, made recommendations, with varying degrees of confidence, for her admission to partnership. Seven of those recommended that she be made partner "with enthusiasm," 14 "with favor," 6 "with mixed emotions, 4 "with negative feelings," and 1 "with mixed emotions/negative feelings." After reviewing the evaluations and conducting interviews, the Associates Committee voted 9-1 not to recommend Evans for full partnership. (Material drawn from the appellate court record.)

APPENDIX B

Recommendations of the Glass Ceiling Commission

Created as part of the Civil Rights Act of 1991, the 21-member bipartisan Glass Ceiling Commission was established to study and recommend ways to eliminate the barriers minorities and women experience when trying to advance into management and decision-making positions in the private sector. Members were appointed by the president and congressional leaders, and the commission was chaired by the secretary of labor. It focused on barriers and opportunities in three areas: (a) the filling of management and decision-making positions, (b) developmental and skill-enhancing activities, and (c) compensation and reward activities. The commission prepared an extensive report on the glass ceiling, titled *A Solid Investment: Making Full Use of the Nation's Human Capital* (1995). In its final act, the commission adopted the following 12 recommendations for business and government to eliminate barriers that keep minority and women out of the top management levels.

The recommendations to business and private firms were

1. Demonstrate CEO commitment
2. Include diversity in all strategic business plans and hold line managers accountable for progress
3. Use affirmative action as a tool
4. Select, promote, and retain qualified individuals
5. Prepare minorities and women for senior positions
6. Educate corporate ranks
7. Initiate work-life and family-friendly policies within firms
8. Adopt high-performance workplace practices

The recommendations to government were

1. Lead by example

2. Strengthen enforcement of antidiscrimination laws
3. Improve data collection
4. Increase disclosure of diversity data

APPENDIX C

U.S. Equal Employment Opportunity Commission— Instructions for Filing a Charge

If you believe you have been discriminated against by an employer, labor union, or employment agency when applying for a job or while on the job because of your race, color, sex, religion, national origin, age, or disability, or believe that you have been discriminated against because of opposing a prohibited practice or participating in an equal employment opportunity matter, you may file a charge of discrimination with the U.S. Equal Employment Opportunity Commission (EEOC).

Charges may be filed in person, by mail, or by telephone by *contacting the nearest EEOC office.* If there is not an EEOC office in the immediate area, call toll free 800-669-4000 for more information. To avoid delay, call or write beforehand if you need special assistance, such as an interpreter, to file a charge.

There are strict time frames in which charges of employment discrimination must be filed. To preserve the ability of EEOC to act on your behalf and to protect your right to file a private lawsuit, should you ultimately need to, adhere to the following guidelines when filing a charge.

Title VII of the Civil Rights Act. Title VII charges must be filed with the EEOC within 180 days of the alleged discriminatory act. However, in states or localities where there is an antidiscrimination law and an agency authorized to grant or seek relief, a charge must be presented to that *state or local* agency. Furthermore, in such jurisdictions, you may file charges with EEOC within 300 days of the discriminatory act, or 30 days after receiving notice that the state or local agency has terminated its processing of the charge, whichever is earlier. It is best to contact EEOC promptly when discrimination is suspected. When charges or complaints are filed beyond these time frames, you may not be able to obtain any remedy.

SOURCE: Equal Employment Opportunity Commission, June 10, 1997 [Online]. Available: http://www.eeoc.gov/facts.

CHAPTER 3

Medical Mentoring

CASE OVERVIEW *The primary subject matter of this case is professional development of women and the potential value of mentoring in that process. A meeting of a group of women physicians provides the setting of this case. Women in medical school and at the initial stages of their careers share with more established women doctors a discussion of the current professional situation of women in medicine, including general practice, highly specialized subfields, and academic medicine. The discussion ranges over a wide variety of problems encountered, with supporting data to document the major points. The case requires a minimal background in organizational culture and professional advancement issues.*

Body of Case

The 40 or so women milled around the conference room until the chair, Ellen Davis, called the session to order. "We are happy, tonight, to have as our invited guests a number of young women who are enrolled in the Orchard University School of Medicine, as well as a number of new practitioners and medical school faculty members. Our chapter of American Medical Women is delighted that you are here. We seek to involve you in our organization, which attempts to serve the special needs of women doctors in our area. Tonight we are especially interested in what problems or concerns you may be facing or worries you

51

have. We hope to design some activities or programs designed especially to address these concerns as a result of tonight's session.

"To help focus our discussion, a panel, representing various medical specialties and positions, has done some initial research on the current experiences of women in their fields. Each panel member will share some findings with us. This will give us a starting point, after which we hope everyone will chime in with information and suggestions for specific actions we might take here in our own chapter.

"Let me first introduce the panel:

Linda Rodriguez is a fourth-year medical student at Orchard U, and she will share some information about the experiences of female medical students;

Marcia Birthright has been in family practice with several other physicians for ten years and is also raising a family of her own;

Amelia Pioneer is a cardiothoracic surgeon and is also on the surgical faculty of Orchard U Medical School; and

Nancy Jenner is a specialist in pediatrics and also serves as chair of the regional chapter of the American Medical Association [AMA].

"We welcome each of you panelists and appreciate the work you have done preparing for tonight's meeting. Linda, let's start with you: What are some of the current issues about women in medical school?"

"Well, Ellen, there is good news and bad news. On the one hand, more women than ever are applying to and being accepted in medical school. There is concern that many young girls are still not encouraged to excel in mathematics and science, especially between the ages of 11 and 15. However, women now constitute over 40% of the student body in medical schools, in contrast to less than 10% in the 1960s and 1970s. The Orchard University Medical School currently has about 38% female students. The increases in female medical students are, of course, related to the quadrupling of women in the profession overall during the past 20 years. As most of you probably know, women now represent 19% of all U.S. physicians, and it is predicted that by the year 2010, 30% of U.S. physicians will be women.

"Many female students in Orchard Med feel that while accepted on the surface, they are not given the same quality of attention and sponsorship that male medical students receive. Furthermore, some of us believe that we are being steered toward certain 'female' specialties and residencies. Both students and faculty seem to have preconceived notions about who 'fits' into which specialty, and some of this seems to relate to gender. The fields most commonly recommended for women are pediatrics, psychiatry, and anesthesiology. Female students feel these fields have an advantage in that women are *already well accepted into them. However, it seems that a number of women feel less free to follow their true preferences, in terms of specialty, than do men. The difficulty of obtaining sponsorship in the fields less populated by women is definitely a factor for many of us.*

"We have formed an association of Women Medical Students and hope to provide some mutual support through that group. In this student group, we are developing a newsletter to share our personal experiences and anecdotes, inviting prominent women physicians to speak to us on a variety of topics, sponsoring an annual retreat, linking with women medical students elsewhere in the country, and exploring connections with the American Medical Women's Association. We also are here tonight because we hope that this group, with all of your experience, may be helpful to us. We are looking forward to hearing what the other members of the panel and the group as a whole have to say about women's current experiences in medicine."

"Thank you, Linda. Your remark about being urged to consider some specialties more than others may relate to some of the research Amelia and Nancy have done about the current status of women in the various specialties. Amelia, as a highly specialized surgeon, how would you respond to Linda's observations?"

"Well, of course I am on the medical school faculty myself, so I certainly hope that would be one contact point for Linda and her peers, if they are interested in cardiology or surgical specialties. I do remember in my own med school years, however, that we women were not encouraged to pursue surgery, in particular, because it was so competitive. The faculty felt that men would make better use of the internships and residencies than women, who might interrupt their careers for family. I know we will return to discuss some family issues, later.

"In terms of specialties, it is clear in data I obtained from the AMA that women more than men concentrate in internal medicine, pediatrics, and family practice. Most women also practice in primary

care situations, dealing directly with patients. Women are still relatively rare in the highly prestigious areas of radiology, surgery, and
cardiology. For example, women were 54% of the residents in pediatrics in 1990, but just 5% of the residents in vascular surgery, one of the
best-paying subspecialties.

"Very few women choose surgery, and this is reflected in my specialty. In 1993, only 2.3% of the residents in cardiothoracic training
were women. In the United States, fewer than 60 women were among
the 5,000 physicians who were board certified in cardiothoracic surgery. At any point in their specialty training or practice, men constitute
more than 95% of cardiothoracic surgeons.

"I know that some women doctors believe that women choose
the primary care fields of their own volition, because they prefer them
for a variety of reasons. Others have argued, however, that women are
forced into these parts of medicine. Dr. Lila A. Wallis, a past president
of the American Medical Women's Association, recently stated that
'women have been pushed into primary care. They aren't always encouraged to go into the high-tech specialties.' This sounds more like
the experience Linda and some of her colleagues seem to be having at
Orchard.

"Some research has suggested that women are particularly good
at providing primary care. A study of medical students in Arizona in
the 1980s indicated that medical students found women physicians
to be 'more sensitive, more altruistic, and less egoistic.' So perhaps
women do seek out these positions because they are well suited for
them. On the other hand, I am not convinced that the great dis-
crepancies in numbers in the various specialties—between men and
women—are primarily due to differences in aptitudes. I suspect there
are still barriers operating here.

"In my own field of cardiothoracic surgery, there are other differences between men and women, besides just their numbers in the
practice. While there are no real differences in background, more men
than women are in university practices, which tend to be more visible
and prestigious. Within universities, there are very different salaries
and almost twice as many men are full professors. Women feel that
promotion practices are often unfair, and men are unlikely to encourage women to pursue this specialty. These findings were from a recent
survey of cardiothoracic surgeons themselves. They certainly confirm

the type of experience that Linda and her peers perceive at Orchard, in terms of the competitive specialties and recruiting for them.

"In academic medicine as a whole, not just surgery, women do far less well than men. I already mentioned differences at the rank of full professor. In 1992, less than 3% of the medical schools were administered by women, and women are less likely than men to move into tenure-track positions in medical schools. Only 24% of the full-time medical school faculty members in 1994 were women. Worse, only 4% of department chairs were women. Many more women are qualified as chairs than have been appointed. Also, in 1994, there were only four women deans of medical schools, although there were 367 women in associate or assistant deanships. (If these women do not advance, we will truly have evidence of a glass ceiling in academic medicine.) A report from the AMA's Council on Ethical and Judicial Affairs in 1993 suggested that women in academic medicine are 'continuing to encounter subtle and overt forms of discrimination during their training and careers.' "

Ellen turned to Nancy, the pediatric specialist on the panel. "Nancy, how do you feel about these differences in numbers of men and women in the various fields, and what have you encountered along these lines, in your own career?"

"Well, Ellen, I'd certainly like to believe I chose pediatrics freely, not because it is a 'woman's field.' Pediatrics is an office-based field, of course, and between 1970 and 1990 women physicians in patient care increased by over 100%, which was largely accounted for by the increase for women physicians in office-based practice. At present, 50.7% of women doctors are office based, which is higher than the number of men, who are more apt to be hospital based. Marcia, who is also in an office-based practice, may also want to comment on this.

"I have an additional concern, however, in my role as chair of the Orchard chapter of the AMA," Nancy continued. "Women have just not achieved leadership positions in our professional groups in numbers that are commensurate with our representation in medicine. Over the years, women physicians have also been less likely to join medical societies such as the AMA, although the American Medical Women's Association, of which we are a part tonight, has a proud tradition.

"As in academic medicine, there is some evidence that women are now beginning to emerge as leaders in professional organizations.

The number of women in the House of Delegates of the AMA has increased from 5% in 1989 to 10% in 1994. Recently, in fact, the first woman chair of the AMA board of trustees, Nancy Dickey, served with distinction. One third of the presidents of state, county, and national medical-specialty societies are women. So progress in this area seems steady, but slow.

"A 'summit' of women leaders in medicine was convened to assess the needs of women doctors, and they cited leadership development as a priority. Perhaps we can discuss some of their other recommendations later, when we get around to talking about action."

"Thank you, Nancy," Ellen said. "I think before opening things up, we should now hear from Marcia Birthright, who is in her tenth year of family practice here in the area. Marcia, what issues do you feel we haven't raised as yet?"

"My concerns, Ellen, have to do with some of the reasons behind the data we have been discussing. I agree with Nancy, that many of us choose office-based and primary care positions freely and because of our aptitudes for these types of practice. Most women physicians are married, half of them to male physicians, and a great majority have children, as I do. I suspect, then, that many women choose office-based work because of its more flexible hours. Women physicians tend to average 55 hours of work per week, compared with the men's average of 61 hours, suggesting that women physicians hold more time in reserve for family concerns. Women also spend more time with each patient. The AMA says that female physicians schedule fewer patients per hour and per week than do their male counterparts.

"Women are about twice as likely as men to be employed by a hospital, HMO, group practice, or other organization. Forty-three percent of women doctors are employees, compared with 22% of men. Just 57% of women doctors work alone, with a partner, as part owner in a group practice, or as an independent contractor. For men doctors, this share is 79%. While independent practitioners generally earn more money, they also tend to work longer hours and must contend with more paperwork and other administrative duties.

"We haven't really discussed earnings much, but of course we all know women doctors earn much less than men, for a variety of factors we have mentioned: They are concentrated in less lucrative specialties; they tend to work fewer hours; they are not as advanced, in academic rank. In 1992, the net average earnings of women averaged 62% of the net earned by men in 1992, according to the AMA. Even among women in practice for 20 or more years, the earnings were 72% of those of men.

"I, myself, am in the midst of juggling my career with high family demands. I have a husband whom I love very much and who loves me very much, and we're very committed to our children and to each other, as well as to our careers. I work a four-day week, which adds up to 40-50 hours per week. My husband and I share grocery shopping, errands, and cooking. We hire some household help, and also have excellent caretakers for the kids. On weekends, when I'm not on call, I'm really with the kids all the time.

"I think this balance would be harder to maintain were I not in practice with another woman physician. We understand each other's needs, and we understand how important family is. I think we are typical of many women physicians who have looked for career opportunities that give us more flexibility. The financial aspects are not superimportant to me. However, I do bristle when my work or career is compared to that of men. As long as you judge me on the basis of hours worked, rather than what I produce, there's no way, as a working mother, I can compete. And I wouldn't say I have the solutions, yet, to the problems of working parents. I often feel I am sort of double-timing everyone in my life. I'm still struggling."

Amelia, the surgeon, chimed in at this point. "That's true for all women physicians, maybe all women professionals. We are being asked to assimilate to the rules that were set up for the '60s male. We are breaking new ground, still. We hope that the field that we enter may be chosen for what we find more interesting, and not be hampered in that decision by questions of male dominance, glass ceilings, and restricted promotions. I think it is also imperative that women, who are doing somewhat better in medical-practice settings, achieve greater prominence in academic and organized medicine."

Ellen turned her attention to the entire group. "I wonder if some of our younger guests would care to respond to any of these informative reports. Do you find yourself troubled or encouraged by what you have heard?"

One of the medical students stirred and began to speak. "I think most of us still in training recognize the reality of the pictures that have been painted here, in terms of the pressures toward primary care and the hesitancy to pursue the more competitive specialties, even if those are the most appealing. I feel drawn toward radiology, yet the faculty in that area are not particularly encouraging, and I don't know who to talk to about my choices, obstacles I might run into, and so on. How can we feel less lonely, and also be professionally realistic in our career assessments and decisions? When I talk to my men friends, they just don't seem to feel these dilemmas in quite the same way."

Nancy Jenner responded eagerly. "The leadership summit of women medical leaders I mentioned earlier agreed with the importance of just those concerns. Those women doctors at the summit recognized the need for support for women physicians; they called for formal structures to provide more effective and consistent, uniform mentoring of women in medicine. Women face the challenge of achieving balance between the overlapping demands of career and personal responsibilities, often more than men do, as we've heard here tonight.

"We all recognize the importance of 'sponsorship' in establishing a successful medical career, and mentoring is an important aspect of that. Also, the summit leaders believed that elements of mentoring and mentoring relationships are characteristically different between men and women; it is often more difficult for women to identify or approach potential mentors. Faculty members who have the potential to serve in this capacity are frequently too busy to assume this role.

"Thus, the summit concluded that multiple strategies need to be developed to increase the number of mentors and to encourage women physicians to seek out these relationships. The need for men as well as women to assume such mentoring responsibilities was emphasized. I think the summit participants are really on to something important, and we should develop a mentoring program."

"I'm not so sure," responded another young doctor. "I have so much to juggle already, I'd hate to waste time just chatting with someone to no particular point."

"What do some of the rest of you think?" asked Ellen. "Is mentoring a possibility we should pursue?"

"We all know how important sponsorship is, early in our careers," responded another. "The acceptable novice physician becomes a sort of 'protégée' of a member of the elite group of established physicians, and thus gets referrals of patients, secures affiliation with the community's most prestigious hospitals, and is offered partnerships and other valuable connections. The initial sponsorship seems to make the new doctor visible to colleagues and gives her a chance to demonstrate competence. As we heard earlier, women are still not represented in some of the more elite inner circles of medicine, so perhaps lack of initial sponsorship or mentoring is one of the hurdles."

"I also think mentoring would help us navigate the family-versus-profession difficulties that have been mentioned. It couldn't hurt to discuss those, especially with other women who've 'been there, done that,' " suggested an additional member.

"But does mentoring really achieve anything?" asked the initial skeptic.

Ellen responded with some additional outside information. "Well, there is currently a national program, sponsored by the Women's Leadership Forum, designed to help 12 already successful women, mostly in business, work with mentors who are even *more* successful women in the same fields. The program is building on the experience of the women who have already overcome barriers in their careers and have come forward to help mentor others. In this Fellows Program, the goal is to identify the obstacles facing the women who are attempting to develop the next stages of their careers. The mentor and 'mentee' work to identify the obstacles, and the mentor shares suggestions for overcoming them. I think this idea might work in medicine, too."

"I have a friend, also in business, in Minnesota, who is at an earlier stage in her career and is participating in a larger mentoring initiative," contributed another.

"This program also was in response to the Glass Ceiling Initiative, which suggested many women hit artificial barriers in their careers. The program brings together 100 'outstanding women' with 100 business leaders in a yearlong, one-on-one relationship. Half the mentors are men and half are women, all volunteers.

"The basic requirements of this program include a 'leadership assessment' of the mentee, including confidential interviews with her manager, peers, and subordinates, followed by a minimum of 14 hours of one-on-one counseling with the mentor; more time may be spent, but participants commit to the 14 hours. The program also provides a total of eight days of training for the mentees, and 'mentoring guidelines' for the mentors, with the advice that mentors should basically use their own experience to guide their mentees. Some of the biggest companies in the Midwest are participating. Initial evaluation suggests this program is providing concrete help to the women involved, and a great many mentors have already indicated their willingness to sign on for another year. I like the clear definition this program seems to have."

One of the medical students seemed interested at this point. "In our Women Medical Students group, we have wondered if there are enough women in the various fields of medicine for us to contact. With small numbers, it seems as if we may need to use a 'group mentoring' approach, where one senior woman relates to a number of younger ones, yet I'm not sure that would be as effective. Or maybe we should follow the Minnesota approach, and use men as mentors also. That would mean less support on the personal issues, though. I'm not sure how I feel about this issue of recruiting the appropriate mentors, and who they are, in medicine."

"Do all the mentors and mentees necessarily have to be in the same location?" queried another student. "Maybe video-conferencing and e-mail, other technology, could be used to link mentors and mentees."

"I also think, later in careers, that a sort of peer-mentoring approach might be useful," said a woman who had been in practice for several years. "I think the linkages need to be with women at similar stages of career advancement, as well as with those more senior. Peers are also good counselors, face similar obstacles, and so on."

"Medical students could also mentor undergraduates, and even girls in the community who are interested in science but short on encouragement and ideas," contributed another student.

"But what's in it for the mentor?" asked a well-established physician. "I think it is important to get our institutions and organizations, associations, hospitals, and so on to recognize the importance of this activity. Several studies have shown that it is important to have unequivocal support of the mentoring concept from the senior management or whoever is important in the leadership of organizations. This gives the mentors encouragement to take the assignment seriously and also allows the professional time needed to carry it out."

"Most of all," added another, "we would need to be very clear about the nature of the mentoring relationship, the responsibilities of both the mentor and the protégée, and the topics that would likely be addressed in the relationship. This lets everyone know what they are getting involved in, and also increases the probability of success, since expectations are clear from the beginning."

"It seems to me that we've accomplished a lot," said Ellen. "We have identified a lot of important issues facing us and other women in medicine. We have also, it seems, reached agreement that a mentoring program would be useful. I'd like to appoint a subcommittee to develop a suggested mentoring program for our chapter to consider. Please address the key issues about mentoring we've examined, plus any others you think are important. These would include:

- A description of the mentoring relationship and the potential benefits for both parties

- The responsibilities of both the mentor and the mentee, the expectations and limitations

- The likely issues to be discussed or addressed in the mentoring relations, given the problems we discussed earlier tonight

- Identification and recruitment of mentors

- Organizational issues, sponsorship, and support for the program

- How and when the mentoring program should be evaluated

"Thank you all very much for coming, and we will look forward to the subcommittee's report."

 Suggested Readings

American Medical Association. (1994). *Report on the Women Physician Leaders Summit*. Chicago: Author.

Braus, P. (1994). How women will change medicine. *American Demographics, 16*, 40.

Dresler, C. M., et al. (1996, November). Experiences of women in cardio-thoracic surgery: A gender comparison. *Archives of Surgery*, pp. 1128-1134.

Eisenberg, C. (1989). Medicine is no longer a man's profession: Or, when the men's club goes coed, it's time to change the regs. *New England Journal of Medicine, 321*, 1542-1544.

Finley, M. (1995). When the doctor is a woman. In *Women like us*, reprinted on the Internet home page of Women In Medicine, University of Texas at Austin.

Fong, K. M. (1995, November 19). Women mentoring women will overcome glass-ceiling barriers. *Los Angeles Times*, p. B-2.

Fried, L. P., Francomano, C. A., MacDonald, S. M., Wagner, E. M., Stokes, E. J., Carbone, K. M., Bias, W. B., Newman, M. M., & Stobo, J. D. (1996). Career development for women in academic medicine: Multiple interventions in a department of medicine. *Journal of the American Medical Association, 276*, 898-905.

Higgins, L. (1994). Mentoring moves mountains. *Stanford Medicine, 11*, 4-8.

Komaromy, M., Bindman, A. B., Haber, R. J., & Sande, M. A. (1993). Sexual harassment in medical training. *New England Journal of Medicine, 328*, 322-326.

Levy, D. (1996, August 6). Women doctors see earnings picture improve. *USA Today* [Online]. Available: http://www.usatoday.com/life/health/hcare/docs/Ihhdo002.htm.

Lorber, J. (1984). *Women physicians*. New York: Tavistock.

Massachusetts Medical Society. (1996). Editorial: Women physicians—Good news and bad news. *New England Journal of Medicine, 334*, 982-983.

Student Response

1. Working in groups assigned by your instructor, develop a mentoring program for the Orchard Chapter of the American Medical Women's Association. Address the issues raised by the chair at the conclusion of the meeting, being sure that your plan includes:

   a description of the mentoring relationship and the potential benefits for both parties;

   the responsibilities of both the mentor and the "mentee," the expectations and limitations;

   the issues likely to be discussed or addressed in the mentoring relationships;

   identification and recruitment of mentors;

   organizational issues, sponsorship, and support for the program; and

   how and when the mentoring program should be evaluated.

2. Develop a presentation of your plan for your class. Assume you are arguing for your plan to the chapter that appointed you to develop it. Your presentation should not exceed 15 minutes, because other proposals will also be made. Use appropriate supporting materials, such as handouts and charts, to summarize your major points.

3. Which of the problems faced by women physicians are best addressed by mentoring? Why?

4. Are there problems faced by women physicians that are not particularly well addressed by mentoring? Why?

5. In your mentoring plan, how do you recommend recruiting the mentors needed for these young women physicians? Do you anticipate any problems in recruitment? How will you "sell" the idea to prospective mentors who, in this case, are already very busy?

6. Given the issues and problems discussed in the case, do you recommend male as well as female mentors in your plan? Why or why not?

7. Do you think the idea of "group mentoring," suggested in the case, would work well in this situation? Why or why not?

8. Do you like the idea of "long distance" mentoring? Why or why not?

9. How would you explain the responsibilities of mentors in your program? Would you place a time limit on the relationship, as was done in the Minnesota plan mentioned in the case?

10. How, and when, will you evaluate this program?

CHAPTER 4

The Pregnant Professor

CASE OVERVIEW *The principals in this case, Karen and Tim, are academics attempting to balance the initial development of two careers with a close personal relationship and starting a family. The case raises the issues of choosing between competing personal and professional demands and needs, as well as the policies that institutions might offer to make this balancing act more feasible. Issues of separation of personal and professional lives are also suggested in the events in the case. The couple in the case also model a rather egalitarian marriage, in terms of career decision making and child care responsibilities.*

Body of Case

"You'd be fools to marry," exclaimed the dean of Arts and Sciences to the two outstanding Ph.D. candidates in front of him. "Do you know how tight the academic job market is? You'll be lucky to find one permanent job, let alone two!"

The two young academics, of course, did not heed this warning. With Tim finished with all his work except the dissertation, and his new spouse, Karen, just ready to begin her dissertation research, the two entered the teaching job market in economics. Hoping to find tenure-track positions in the same location, they were sadly disappointed. Tim accepted a first position in New York City, whereas Karen landed a position in a prestigious university in the Midwest.

"We were groomed," she later said, "in graduate school to take the 'best' position, in the most prestigious department. We assumed this would lead to better pay, working conditions, students, and all the rest. I guess I was pretty naive not to ask more questions." Thus the couple began a three-year period of commuting between New York and the Midwest.

"I was wary of putting my career on hold to follow Tim," Karen explained, "because I had seen other couples start out a marriage with great intentions of equality, only to resort to gender roles when real decisions had to be made." No definite limits were placed on the length of time they would commute, and they had no real plan for terminating the commuting arrangement.

"Both of us found our jobs more difficult than we had ever really imagined," Tim reported later. "I didn't much like teaching, and it took up so much time that I didn't finish my dissertation in the first year, as I'd planned." Karen did finish her dissertation during her first year at Midwest University, but felt she compromised its quality due to departmental pressure to finish it and actively publish other work. But the commuting was hard on them both. "Having two stressful jobs without the daily support of the other person was a drag," Karen admits.

Thus, after three years, Tim quit his eastern position and relocated to the Midwest. The university was located in a state capital, and he obtained a position as a policy analyst. About the same time, Karen discovered she was pregnant. She had wanted a child and had worried about delaying pregnancy due to infertility problems in her family. But she knew that a pregnancy would complicate her life in an academic department where professors "were supposed to work all the time and never have a life." She recalled being told by one of the tenured faculty that if she had an outside interest she shouldn't tell anyone about it, as they would think that she wasn't serious about academia. Still, "I knew I wanted a child and I didn't want to take the risk of waiting until my career was on more solid ground—which it wasn't at the time, as it was taking me a while to get my research published."

As it turned out, Karen was fired during the second trimester of her pregnancy. The university had yearly contracts for its assistant professors (something she had not asked about when applying for her position). The previous year, the department had been quite critical of her, not the quality of her work but the quantity and the speed with which she was getting things published. They decided during her fourth year that she surely would not achieve tenure in the sixth year, so they would terminate her before the tenure decision point. (It was, she described, a "general bloodletting," as three assistant professors were terminated.)

"I thought it was sleazy," she shared with a friend, "as I was not told until the week I was fired that this was even a possibility. There were several possibilities to stop the tenure clock (which would allow more time before the tenure decision), if all they were worried about was time. First, anytime one went on unpaid leave the tenure clock could stop; when I interviewed, they made constant reference to this policy. So I could have been allowed to take leave. Second, the university was in the process of adopting a policy of stopping the tenure clock when an assistant professor had a baby. But both these policies were ignored by my department and I was fired."

Karen realized she might have sued Midwest University, but reported that she did not have the emotional energy to do so. She was also filled with self-doubt, questioning her own dedication to the academic life, after a very successful career as an undergraduate and graduate student. So she "retreated" and accepted a part-time, temporary position in state government, during which she hoped to redefine her career goals and strategies. This occurred when her baby was about six months old.

Meanwhile, Tim was learning a lot in his own government position. He had mastered writing regulations, writing effectively, negotiating with many different types of people, and working in a bureaucracy. He was, however, working about 60 hours a week, in addition to sharing care of the couple's infant daughter. He couldn't seem to get any writing done, and his dissertation languished as a result. He found himself open to the idea of another change.

Karen reported another problem with Tim's government job. "My husband's office was terrible about recognizing the demands of having a new baby. We came home from the hospital on Wednesday and one of Tim's coauthors wanted him to come to a meeting on Friday. When Friday rolled around, I just told Tim not to go, to say that he couldn't leave me alone. (This wasn't really true, but I'll lie when I have to.) He already had a big meeting, with lots of required preparation, on Sunday and Monday. It was a crazy time, and I'm not sure how he did it."

While finishing at the university and later working in her temporary job, Karen was also conducting research with a colleague at a small, liberal arts college nearby. Karen observed that this colleague had more "people contact" and personal freedom than Karen had experienced at Midwest University and was also energized by her contact with undergraduate students and colleagues in many different academic disciplines.

"I had figured out that what stifled me at Midwest University was the lack of energy I got from other people, from my work environment itself," she reflects. "I was supposed to sit in my office, or the library, or my apartment, all day, all by myself doing research, and I just couldn't do it. It drove me nuts; I needed to get energy from the people and place around me. (Earlier when I had complained to the department chair about the lack of any intellectual exchange at Midwest, he said to me, 'Well, this is not a social club.') I also didn't like the narrowness of the research university, the concentration on our own narrow specialties to the exclusion of everything else. It was the connections between my work and the 'everything else' that made academic work interesting to me."

A mentor, a female colleague in another department, at Midwest University was another influence on Karen during this transitional period. The news that female assistant professors were leaving the university at a higher rate than male assistant professors had provided the impetus to establish a mentoring program for women professors.

Karen reports: "I was hooked up with a woman in another department who was absolutely fantastic. I requested someone with children, and she understood what was going on, so I didn't have to justify or defend myself. She also let me know that my department at Midwest didn't have to act the way it did, that other departments at the university would have made other decisions. She helped me with my vita, and she told me I should feel comfortable applying for any job I wanted.

"I decided a liberal arts college might be better for me, too," Karen states. "I was in somewhat of a panic, as I had nothing lined up. I felt like I was jumping into the great unknown. I worried about it, but it was also somewhat freeing. I didn't have to worry about what other people would think about me, or what they wanted me to do, I only had to figure out what I wanted."

Eventually, Karen did look for a liberal arts faculty position. She reported that she was "picky" about choosing a desirable location, for herself and her family, as well as a school with a good reputation and working conditions.

"I was willing to stay in academia, but only on my own terms," she points out. "I wasn't willing to 'settle' for a mediocre school or position. On the other hand, in my temporary government job I had missed the intellectual life of academia—the supposing, and hypothesizing, and playing with ideas. So I went back on the job market."

The first year there were no positions that met Karen's criteria. The second year she was lucky, however: There were six liberal arts jobs in places acceptable to her and to Tim, and she was offered a desirable one. "Tim was very supportive," Karen recalls. "If we moved to Worth, he could spend some time finishing his dissertation. He also thought the job was a good one for me. He liked the idea of living in New England, where Worth was located. He was willing to move without even seeing the place. I, on the other hand, was wary and risk averse. I was worried about what would happen if I didn't like Worth, or Worth didn't like me. We'd be stuck out there, with no obvious way of getting out. I also didn't want to spend five to seven years putting down roots in one place, only to have to move if I were denied tenure. Tim talked me into it."

At the time of this move to Worth College, the couple's child was two years old. They "bought as much child care as they could afford" so that Tim could work on completing his dissertation; he also did some part-time consulting for his previous employer in the Midwest, which eased his transition to their new location. Karen, meanwhile, started her tenure clock over at Worth, even though she had taught for four years at Midwest university and published a book and a batch of articles that she felt "was enough to be an associate professor just about anyplace."

"I didn't mind starting the tenure process over, as it took the immediate pressure off. I considered myself 'mommy-tracked' even though no one ever said that to me, and I never told anyone else that that's what I was doing," Karen states. She found the demands of teaching in a small college intense and time-consuming.

"To manage my time, I came up with several tricks, like slotting so much time for preparing for class and not spending any more time than that on preparation, or having a quota of papers to grade every day in order to get them done on time. But I think the most important decision I ever made was to live my life now, as opposed to waiting until I got tenure to have a life, and just accept the consequences. I would stay in academia on my terms."

She found Worth somewhat more hospitable to her terms. "Many of the faculty here have small children and expect to spend time with them," she said of the college. "I see little kids at work quite often, and no one blinks an eye when I show up with mine. Because it's a small college, far from a big city, I think it probably attracts people who want to have children and spend time with them. Midwest University was terrible on this score. We never heard about anybody having a life outside of work, and certainly, I didn't see children at the office."

In both positions, however, Karen found there are many extra-curricular expectations of professors. "There are many after-hours meetings and dinners—work as socializing. I will do some of these, and refuse others, depending on what is going on at home and how much I have been away recently."

Tim took a couple of years to finish his dissertation. Just as Karen was due to go on "assistant professor leave"—a year provided at half salary so assistant professors can take a full year's leave in their fourth year, prior to the tenure decision—Tim found a great job in a nearby state capital as a research fellow at the Economics Institute. This is an hour away from Worth, but Tim and Karen both report that "since Worth is in the middle of nowhere" they feel pretty fortunate. It is common for spouses of Worth faculty not to find jobs. As Karen ironically points out, "This mostly applies to women, of course; it seems like when it's the man who can't find work, the couple moves away." And Tim adds that it was the kind of job he really wanted to have, one that eventually might take him back to state government, which is a possible future goal.

During Karen's assistant professor leave she started thinking about having another child. She was ambivalent, mainly because she hated being pregnant, and being a pregnant assistant professor at Midwest University had drastically complicated her life. She spent a lot of time talking with other female faculty friends about when they should have children—would it hurt them if they got pregnant now or later, should they take maternity leave, who could they talk to about their decisions, and similar questions. Karen wrestled with her own questions. Should she wait until she came up for tenure to have another baby? She was already in her late 30s, and waiting just made it more unlikely that she would get pregnant. But if she became pregnant while an untenured assistant professor, how would she manage? What would happen? Could she risk her job security a second time, after all she and Tim had already been through?

 Suggested Readings

Feldman, C. (1997). *I work too: Working wives talk about their dual-career lives.* Santa Barbara, CA: Blue Point.

Friedman, D. E. (1990). Work and family: The new strategic plan. *Human Resource Planning, 13*(2), 79-89.

Gilbert, L. A. (1993). *Two careers/one family.* Newbury Park, CA: Sage.

Karsten, M. F. (1994). Balancing career and family/personal life. In M. F. Karsten, *Management and gender: Issues and attitudes* (pp. 157-183). Westport, CT: Praeger.

Schwartz, F. (1989, January/February). Management women and the new facts of life. *Harvard Business Review,* pp. 65-76.

Student Response

1. What is the difference between a dual-career and a dual-earner couple? Which apply to Karen and Tim?

2. Should work life and family/personal life be integrated or separated? Explain. How did Karen and Tim approach this issue?

3. What are the advantages and disadvantages of a dual-career relationship? How is it different from a couple who have a dual-earner relationship?

4. What expectations of their employers created the most problems for Tim and Karen? Do you think these are common in other professions?

5. What does Karen mean when she says she considered herself "mommy-tracked"? Do you think mommy tracks are a good idea or not? Why? What is the purpose of mommy tracks?

6. What institutional policies might have helped Tim and Karen pursue both their careers and their desire for a family? Do you think their employers' attitudes were typical of the 1990s workplace or not, in terms of family policies? (See the appendixes to the case for some relevant policy information.)

7. Given what the case reveals about Karen's and Tim's priorities, do you think they should have another child now, or not? Why?

APPENDIX A

Summary of the Family and Medical Leave Act of 1993

The Family and Medical Leave Act of 1993 (FMLA) became effective August 5, 1993. The FMLA requires employers of 50 or more employees within a 75-mile area to provide up to 12 weeks of unpaid, job-protected leave to eligible employees for certain family and medical reasons. Employees are eligible if they have worked for a covered employer for at least one year and for 1,250 hours over the previous 12 months.

Reason for Taking Leave

An employer must grant unpaid leave to an eligible employee for one or more of the following reasons:

- For the care of the employee's child (birth, or placement for adoption or foster care)

- For the care of the employee's spouse, son or daughter, or parent, who has a serious health condition

- For a serious health condition that makes the employee unable to perform his or her job

The employee may be required to provide advance leave notice and medical certification.

Job and Benefits Protection

Upon return from FMLA leave, most employees must be restored to their original or equivalent positions with equivalent pay, benefits, and other employment terms. The use of FMLA leave cannot result in the loss of any employment benefit that accrued prior to the start of an employee's leave.

SOURCE: Excerpted from U.S. Department of Labor, Wage and Hour Division [Online]. Available: http://www.dol.gov.

APPENDIX B

Facts About
Pregnancy Discrimination

The Pregnancy Discrimination Act is an amendment to Title VII of the Civil Rights Act of 1964. Discrimination on the basis of pregnancy, childbirth, or related medical conditions constitutes unlawful sex discrimination under Title VII. Women affected by pregnancy or related conditions must be treated in the same manner as other applicants or employees with similar abilities or limitations.

Hiring

An employer cannot refuse to hire a woman because of her pregnancy-related condition as long as she is able to perform the major functions of her job. An employer cannot refuse to hire her because of its prejudices against pregnant workers or the prejudices of co-workers, clients, or customers.

Pregnancy and Maternity Leave

An employer may not single out pregnancy-related conditions for special procedures to determine an employee's ability to work. However, an employer may use any procedure used to screen other employees' ability to work. For example, if an employer requires its employees to submit a doctor's statement concerning their inability to work before granting leave or paying sick benefits, the employer may require employees affected by pregnancy-related conditions to submit such statements.

If an employee is temporarily unable to perform her job due to pregnancy, the employer must treat her the same as any other temporarily disabled employee, for example, by providing modified tasks, alternative assignments, disability leave, or leave without pay.

Pregnant employees must be permitted to work as long as they are able to perform their jobs. If an employee has been absent from work as a result of a pregnancy-related condition and recovers, her employer may not require her to remain on leave until the baby's birth. An employer may not have a rule that prohibits an employee from returning to work for a predetermined length of time after childbirth.

Employers must hold open a job for a pregnancy-related absence the same length of time jobs are held open for employees on sick or disability leave.

SOURCE: U.S. Equal Employment Opportunity Commission [Online]. Available: http://www.eeoc.gov/facts/fs-preg.html.

APPENDIX C

Relevant Policies, Midwest University and Worth College

Midwest University's Policy Regarding the "Tenure Clock" and Childbirth

Requests for extension of the probationary period (the period prior to granting of tenure) with respect to childbirth or adoption shall be submitted by the faculty member in writing to the vice chancellor for Academic Affairs (with informational copies to the faculty member's department chair and dean) within one year of the birth or adoption. Approval of the request for an extension of up to one year is presumed. The vice chancellor will notify the faculty member, department chair, and dean of the action taken.

More than one request may be granted because of responsibilities with respect to childbirth or adoption where more than one birth or adoption occurs during the probationary period. Where a leave of absence of six weeks or more has been granted for childbirth or adoption within one year of the birth or adoption, the total resulting extensions of the probationary period, for each birth or adoption, may not exceed one year.

Worth College's Assistant Professor Leave Policy

Worth has a program of leaves for assistant professors that provides a one-semester leave with support equivalent to full pay, for any eligible assistant professor who is deemed to have a worthy research or other creative project best supported by released time from teaching. Eligibility is restricted to assistant professors who have been reappointed to a four-year second term or whose initial appointments were for a term of more than three years. . . . Such leaves are most often granted in the person's fourth year at the college. . . . Assistant professors are expected to apply for grant funds available outside the college to help support the leave. . . . Should the assistant professor so wish, it may be possible to combine outside funding or a leave without pay with an assistant professor leave, in order to achieve a full-year leave of absence.

(Note: This policy was *not* in effect during Karen's service at Midwest University.)

CHAPTER 5

Sexual Harassment in the Army

CASE OVERVIEW *This case presents descriptions of sexual harassment in the U.S. Army from two perspectives: (a) reports based on actual individual incidents that surfaced in the mid-1990s, and (b) Defense Department survey data assessing the extent of sexual harassment in the military in the 1980s and 1990s. The case emphasizes the difficulties of changing an organizational culture that tolerates sexual harassment.*

The chapter begins with a description of reported incidents of rape on an Army training base in the mid-1990s, presented through the victim's reports of what occurred. The context of these incidents is the superior-subordinate relationship between male drill sergeants and new female trainees. The case proceeds with the reporting of numerous similar incidents, throughout the Army, during the same time period. Historical survey data are presented next, indicating that sexual harassment is not a new problem in the Army.

 Body of Case

Jennifer Bostrom, 18, is solidly built, 5 feet 3 inches tall and 134 pounds, with a firm jaw, blond hair, and brown eyes. She joined the Army straight out of high school in Iowa and did basic training at Fort Leonard Wood. She was sent to Albemarle Proving Ground several months later and assigned to Charlie Company.

77

Ms. Bostrom reports that, early in her training, a drill sergeant in her company, Nolan Beane, had been spending the night in the barracks. "My roommate was asleep," she said. "He said I had to go down to his office." She said Beane had induced her to have illegal sexual intercourse in his office—not actual rape, she said, but she had thought she had to acquiesce. It is against military rules for superior officers to fraternize with their charges.

After a month, she found someone in whom she could confide—Staff Sergeant Olivia Winn, one of the school's seven women among 39 drill sergeants. Sgt. Winn helped drive Ms. Bostrom's complaint up the chain of command.

Then, one day, Ms. Bostrom was sent to Alpha Company to copy some papers and ran into another drill sergeant, Alan Simmons. She said he had ordered her into an office latrine and had told her to have sex with him on the floor. "When he got through," she said, "he was like: 'Get out. Don't get in my face.' "

Some months later, word began to leak of numerous allegations of sexual harassment and abuses at Albemarle. Ms. Bostrom was the only accuser to come forward publicly. "Most people don't talk to me," she said. "They can't believe I said something because it draws negative attention to the Army. They say I asked for it. I didn't say no." Shortly after these remarks, Ms. Bostrom attempted suicide. She was taken to Walter Reed military hospital, and subsequently granted an honorable discharge.

The Tip of the Iceberg

Twenty-six women ultimately submitted formal allegations against Drill Sergeant Simmons, ten of whom alleged rape. One reason the women did not complain earlier, post attorneys said, is that Simmons's company commander, Captain Dale Ronis, was also preying on the trainees. The captain, whose plea has not been made public, was later to be tried on rape charges, as well. The situation was a graphic example of one of the biggest obstacles the Army faces in ridding its ranks of sexual misconduct: the inherent vulnerability of low-ranking soldiers in a closed, hierarchical organization.

Many described this base as a place where the strict chain of command broke down. They stated that drill sergeants and trainees alike routinely initiated consensual sexual relations—a violation of military law—and that charges of sexual abuse and rape went unreported and apparently undetected, despite an elaborate counseling system set up by the Army. The strict rules governing social behavior between the sexes apparently were broken, and no one was held accountable.

The power of drill sergeants appeared to be significantly related to the problems at Albemarle. Drill sergeants are entrusted with absolute authority over young recruits, who must obey their every order, no matter how unreasonable it may seem. The relationship is supposed to be so formal that drill sergeants are forbidden to have even a social conversation with trainees, yet so intimate that the drill sergeants often serve as surrogate parents, guidance counselors, and mentors who must be aware of any personal problems or difficulties with adjustment that their trainees are facing. The men accused at Albemarle appeared to have violated both of these aspects of the drill sergeant's typical role.

Although these incidents were initially attributed to a "few bad apples," the charges later reverberated throughout the Army. After the first reports from Albemarle, the Army's Criminal Investigation command opened a hotline to permit women to buck the chain of command and make their complaints directly. Only months after the hotline began, 20 or 30 sergeants and a captain were accused at Albemarle by at least 50 different women.

At other bases as well, a flood of charges came forth. At Fort Jackson, near Columbia, South Columbia, 64 people were punished for sexual misconduct occurring in a two-year period. At Fort Leonard Wood in Missouri, 28 instructors were placed under investigation for sexual misconduct; two drill sergeants were discharged and given prison terms for illegal sex with nine female recruits. Only 12 weeks after the hotline was created in 1997, the Army had recorded 7,000 calls alleging sexual harassment.

Investigations by the Army higher command and the Armed Services Committees of the U.S. Congress explored the reasons for the problem and why it had gone undetected previously. Some earlier surveys should have indicated problems. In 1980, 150 of 300 women in the Third Infantry Division in Germany reported that they were subject to unwanted physical advances. Two broad Pentagon inquiries then found systemic misconduct in all the services, including instructor-trainee abuses at Fort Mead, Maryland, much like those later reported at Albemarle.

In 1988, 64% of 20,000 women surveyed had said they had received unwanted sexual attention in the previous year; by a 1995 survey, that percentage had dropped to 55%. Seventy-eight percent of the 90,000 military personnel surveyed in 1995 said they had faced objectionable behavior, 70% were targets of crude behavior, and 63% encountered sexist behavior and attitudes. Some in the Army felt encouraged that sexual harassment seemed to have declined since the 1988 survey, but senior defense officials still considered the findings unacceptably high.

"Why Didn't We Know About This?"

An analysis of the 1995 survey results struck other somber notes. Among other things, it found that most women kept their complaints to themselves, in many cases because they thought nothing would be done. Many respondents said that their complaints had been met with ridicule, retaliation, or indifference, a charge repeated in interviews with Army women at Albemarle and elsewhere.

In all the armed services, very few of the women who reported harassment behind the anonymity of surveys filed formal complaints. Between 1991 and 1997, the Army received about 1,200 complaints from women each year, proportionately about the same as the other military services. Among Army women who said they had reported harassment, 56% said that they had been urged to drop the complaint or had not been taken seriously, that their supervisor had received the report with hostility, or that no action had been taken. Just 27% said the person harassing them had been counseled to stop or had been transferred. One fifth of the women said they believed that they had received a lower performance rating as a result of complaining. Investigation also has shown that the Army throws out almost two thirds of the complaints as unsustainable, far more than the other services.

Army women also reported the lowest expectations of any of the military services that their leadership would intervene in sexual harassment situations. A majority of Army women surveyed said they did not believe their military leaders were making "honest and responsible efforts to stop sexual harassment."

Summoned before the Senate Armed Services Committee to testify about the scandal at the training grounds, the Secretary of the Army assured the committee that the Army was pursuing a "zero tolerance" policy against sexual harassment. But critics fault the Army's culture and structure for the scope of the problem. Harassment cases under an officer's command can hinder chances of advancement, and Army officials appear to be particularly hostile to complaints of abuse. "At some posts, they are not reporting the rapes," said Suellen Barnett, a military law attorney in Denver. Post commanders "don't want those statistics," she said.

Another problem, critics pointed out, is that the Army chaplains, considered to be "neutral parties" to whom soldiers can take complaints, have become hard to find because their numbers have shrunk with budget cuts. At Albemarle, the sole chaplain had been reassigned to a teaching job.

Women's groups also say the Army has made only perfunctory efforts to tackle the problem. They note that the antiharassment task force formed in 1996, like earlier ones, was made up almost entirely of senior and retired Army men and women who rose through the ranks of the institution they managed and are now investigating. Objectivity is difficult for such a group to achieve.

Another issue in the Army inquiries had been whether those found guilty of wrongdoing are held accountable. Several of those accused in the Albemarle events faced courts-martial. Some noncommissioned officers appear to have been given administrative punishment and then reassigned, according to a 1993 Army memo.

One commander faulted some top commanders of Army training facilities for not acting more decisively. "You've got to have certain high, moral ethical standards if you're going to combat sexual harassment," said Lt. Col. Wesly Flanigan, now retired. "But when you get to the higher ranks, everything turns gray and gets political. There is also evidence that officers help to cover up these incidents."

What is reported to have occurred at Albemarle, then, although apparently extreme, illustrates the difficulty the Army has long had in dealing with allegations of sexual misconduct. Rep. June Housman, a member of a House subcommittee that has investigated sexual misconduct in the armed forces, said the Albemarle cases suggested that Army antiharassment programs "may not have accomplished much of anything at all." Secretary of the Army Togo West was, however, determined to address the problem squarely, and wanted to begin with changes in training. He believed that this is the point at which to attack the Army's culture of tolerance for sexual harassment.

The question is: What sorts of training should be instituted? Second, is Secretary West correct in assuming that training is the best way to address the Army's problem? What other options might he pursue?

 Suggested Readings

Army unveils report on sex harassment scandal. (1997, September 7). *New York Times* [Online, Top of the News]. Available: http://archives.nytimes.com.

Collins, E. C., & Blodgett, T. B. (1981, March/April). Sexual harassment: Some see it . . . some won't. *Harvard Business Review* (pp. 76-95).

Graham, B. (1996, June 15). At least half of military women face harassment, despite falloff. *Washington Post* [Online]. Available: http://www.washingtonpost.com/wp-adv/archives.

Greenhouse, L. (1998, June 27). High court clarifies law on workplace sexual harassment. *New York Times* [Online]. Available: http://archives.nytimes.com.

Harris v. Forklift Systems, Inc., 114 S.Ct. 367 (1993).

Meritor Savings Bank, FSB v. Vinson, 106 S.Ct. 2399 (1986).

Priest, D. (1997, January 12). Wrongdoing up command chain. *Washington Post* [Online]. Available: http://www.washingtonpost.com/wp-adv/archives.

Priest, D. (1997, December 16). Panel urges separate military training for men, women. *Washington Post* [Online]. Available: http://www.washingtonpost.com/wp-adv/archives.

Sciolino, E. (1997, April 15). Rape witnesses tell of base out of control. *New York Times* [Online]. Available: http://archives.nytimes.com.

Stuart, P. (1991). Prevent sexual harassment in your work force. *Personnel Journal, 70*(12), 34.

U.S. Merit System Protection Board. (1995, October). *Sexual harassment in the federal workplace: Trends, progress, continuing challenges.* Washington, DC: Government Printing Office.

Student Response

1. Do you agree that Secretary West is correct in focusing on training as the priority means for addressing sexual harassment in the Army? Why or why not?

2. What should be the content of sexual harassment training in the Army? Working with a group, develop a set of recommendations for sexual harassment training for the Army.

3. What unique features of the Army as an organization seem to be making the elimination of sexual harassment more difficult than anticipated when efforts addressing the problem first began?

4. Why were women in the Army so reluctant to report harassment, and how can this be changed?

5. Sexual harassment has been defined by the Supreme Court as including a "hostile work environment" (see Appendix A), as well as overt sexual behaviors. How might a hostile environment be related to the incidents described in this case?

APPENDIX A

Definitions of Sexual Harassment

Sexual harassment is a form of sex discrimination that violates Title VII of the Civil Rights Act of 1964 (and the 1991 amendments to that act).

"*Unwelcome* sexual advances, requests for sexual favors, and other verbal or physical conduct of a *sexual nature* constitute sexual harassment when submission to or rejection of this conduct *explicitly or implicitly affects an individual's employment,* unreasonably interferes with an individual's work performance, or creates an intimidating, *hostile, or offensive work environment*" (U.S. Equal Employment Opportunity Commission, 1997 [Online]. Available: http://www.eeoc.gov; italics added).

The key concepts in harassment thus are as follows: the sexual nature of the behavior; its unwelcome nature; intent versus impact of the behavior (impact is what matters); inappropriate use of power; and the "reasonable person standard"—meaning the behavior is offensive to a reasonable person—used by the courts in "hostile environment" cases.

There are two broad categories of sexual harassment: *quid pro quo* ("this for that") harassment and *hostile environment* harassment.

Quid pro quo harassment often involves:

- Employment decisions or expectations that are implicitly or explicitly based on the employee giving or denying sexual favors

- The person initiating the behavior is positioned with the authority to make job-related threats or promises

- Employment decisions affected could include hiring decisions, salary increases, shift schedules, work assignments, performance expectations, among others

Examples are demanding sexual favors in return for the promise of a raise; firing someone because they ended a relationship with the supervisor; changing job performance ratings for refusing to date the manager.

Hostile environment sexual harassment incorporates the following:

■ The behavior focuses on the sexuality of another person or occurs because of the person's gender

■ The behavior is severe or pervasive enough that it interferes with job performance or the atmosphere is considered abusive

■ A "reasonable person" would also have been offended

■ Anyone in the workplace can participate in the behavior, including both men and women, agents of the employer, co-workers, nonemployees frequently at the work site, and so on

Examples are sexual jokes; sexual comments; sexual pictures, cartoons; leering, staring; lewd gestures; excessive romantic attention; repeated requests for dates; touching, including brushing, hugging, patting, pinching, rubbing; groping, grabbing, fondling; sexual assault; rape. All of the above are harassment if they are serious, pervasive, and unwelcome.

Conclusion

Five Issues, or Maybe Just One?

Betty Friedan, the founder of the National Organization for Women, is widely credited with igniting the modern women's movement with the publication in 1963 of *The Feminine Mystique.* In discussing the "problem that has no name," this early work defined the challenges of women at midcentury, as they struggled for equality in a variety of spheres, and the development of fulfilling lives of their own. Ms. Friedan's recent work, *Beyond Gender: The New Politics of Work and Family* (1997), argues that America's *current* workplace problems seriously threaten the health of families and require a new paradigm of work and family life. Economic justice, rather than "narrow identity politics," is the basis for women's and men's continued progress toward equality in the 1990s, she argues, and for the just treatment of children in society, as well. The notions of work equity and gender reflected in these two works—more than 30 years apart—provide an illuminating backdrop to the specific gender and workplace issues raised here. In particular, the complex interconnections between issues of workplace equity and the nature of family life are becoming clear.

The cases in this volume have each illustrated one area of gender concern in the contemporary workplace. In reality, however, the five categories of issues included are very intertwined and affect each other in a myriad of most significant ways. A brief review of the basic

components of each situation included in the cases will make this
point clear.

In "Half a Pie, or None?" Kirsten Andersen sought to advance
her already successful professional life to the level of top management
in a major corporation. She intended to do this by acquiring a specific
set of new skills and experience, which she believed would then lead
logically to top management positions. Her immediate problem, as
described in the case, was pervasive gender stereotyping of the specific work she sought. Her situation, however, reflects several other
gender-related workplace issues, as well. For example, her inability to
move into an evaluator's position effectively blocked the advancement she sought into the management level; in this way she was
encountering a sort of glass ceiling within the organization. In addition, her career-planning efforts appeared to be done entirely on her
own; at no point did she seem to have effective mentoring available.
Her strongest organizational supporter, Mr. Green, seemed relatively
ineffective when her crises developed, although she did continue to
seek his advice. Finally, although there was certainly no overt sexual
harassment in this case, it is possible that the strict stereotyping of
work in the organization was related to other behaviors that might
constitute a "hostile environment."

In the second case, Meghan Evans, in her attempts to achieve a
legal partnership, most obviously wrestled with the possible existence
of a glass ceiling in her firm, which is primarily a compensation/
promotion issue. However, issues of career development and mentoring were also very relevant to Meghan's experience. The support of
partners is clearly critical to achieving a legal partnership, and it is
unclear whether Meghan had staunch supporters. No partners appeared in the case as active advisers to Meghan, possibly indicating a
dearth of mentoring for her. The assignment of "prominent" cases is
also a career development issue raised in the case. In addition, Meghan
is charged with the financial and emotional responsibility of her two
children. Although the case does not suggest that this family role complicated her legal work, it is certainly possible that it did. The six-year
time frame for achieving partnership might have conflicted with the
responsibilities of parenting in a variety of ways, depending on the
ages of Meghan's children during that period and their particular
situations and needs. Potential sexual harassment is also included in

Meghan's situation, in the references to offensive behavior of several attorneys in the firm. The attempt to change Meghan's area of legal expertise to family law may also indicate a problem of gender stereotyping within her firm. Thus, although Meghan's case is an interesting example of potential glass ceiling issues and their complexity, each of the other gender-related issues may also be present in her workplace environment and may affect her progress toward the partnership she seeks.

The physicians in "Medical Mentoring" were also subject to a complex interplay of gender issues. The focus of their discussion was on the need for early sponsorship into desirable specialties and positions, and the difficulties they faced in acquiring this essential mentoring and assistance from senior physicians. They had also encountered issues related to compensation and advancement, however, as they debated at some length the reasons for their earnings being less than those of male physicians, and the difficulties of advancing into the top positions of medical school faculty and administration. Clearly, balancing family responsibilities with the demands of the practice of medicine was also difficult for many of these women. Sexual harassment, although not mentioned in this case, is present in the experiences of female medical students, as documented by Dr. Miriam Komaromy and published in the *New England Journal of Medicine* (Komaromy, Bindman, Haber, & Sande, 1993). Here, again, the gender issues affecting these women doctors are complex and interconnected.

Tim and Karen, the academic couple in "The Pregnant Professor," also encountered a mix of gender issues in their early work and family experiences. The focus of their case was clearly on the competing pressures they experienced from combining their chosen academic and policy careers with establishing a young family. Karen also needed help, however, in defining (and redefining) her long-term career goals, and the availability of a mentor for even a brief period appeared important in helping her to revise her career goals. Her husband also made several career-planning readjustments in the time period included in the case, although it is unclear whether he received mentoring as an aid in that process. (Interestingly, their *initial* mentor in graduate school, an academic, appeared in a most discouraging light, essentially telling them both that their careers and marriage were incompatible.) Advancement issues also applied to Karen's situation, as she struggled with the high expectations for tenure at Midwest University and the informal culture of her department regarding "having a life" and commitment to work.

Finally, "Sexual Harassment in the Army," while graphically documenting the extent and nature of sexual harassment, also raises issues of career development and advancement, as well as the need for a sort of mentoring. It is clear that the primary victim of the harassment in the case seeks a female drill sergeant in whom to confide, an indication of the need of a younger woman for the support and advice of a more senior one. The low numbers of women drill sergeants also reflect a possible gender stereotyping of that position, or even a glass ceiling barrier to entering that position.

Although family concerns are not raised in the case, it is certainly arguable that the structure of military careers and assignments is still quite difficult to combine with the role of wife and mother, especially if the individuals involved retain a fairly traditional definition of those roles. Research indicates, for example, that one of the major reasons, among both men and women, for denying relocation of work assignments is the perceived impact on their families (Garland, 1991). It is entirely possible, then, that a woman encountering sexual harassment in the Army might also be affected by issues of career development and mentoring, promotion and compensation issues, balancing family roles with a military career, and possible gender stereotyping of potential assignments. Her choices about one of these issues—here, sexual harassment—could both affect and be affected by the others.

Friedan's phrase, "the problem that has no name," became a shorthand phrase for the issues of gender equality in the 1960s and 1970s. Although subsequent analysis and discussion of gender issues have become more precise and detailed, it is possible that lumping the issues together has real validity. For, as seen in these few cases, the gender issues in the contemporary workplace are inextricably intertwined. Furthermore, as Friedan's recent work would suggest, these issues affect the work and personal lives of men as well as women and, increasingly, their children, as well. So perhaps, after all, it is *one* problem—albeit one with many facets—as Friedan argues in *Beyond Gender*.

Organizational Culture

The cases here point out another significant feature of gender issues in the workplace. The specific nature of a particular issue, the form it takes, and the options and means available for addressing it are different in various types of organizations and informal work cultures. Of special value in understanding how organizational culture develops, can be recognized, and changes, is Edgar Schein's (1985) important work, *Organizational Culture and Leadership*. Briefly examining Schein's premises provides a basis for examining the importance of organizational culture in the gender-related workplace issues addressed here.

Leaders in organizations, according to Schein, create the culture of those organizations, initially. Subsequently, however, the culture is "owned" by the organization, and then the culture helps create new leaders. When organizations experience major difficulties or "adaptive problems," the leaders must step outside the prevailing culture to start the process of change. This, if successful, redefines the part of the culture that is nonfunctional or problematic.

Organizational culture is defined by Schein (1985) as containing the following elements: patterns of interaction, basic norms of behavior, the espoused values of the group, its formal philosophy, the "rules of the game" or "ropes" in the organization, the atmosphere or climate of work and the feelings related to that, shared meanings, and integrating symbols of the organization (pp. 8, 9). A culture exists in an organization when a group has enough shared history to form a set of shared assumptions (p. 12). Schein also asserts that if leaders are not "conscious of the cultures in which they are embedded, those cultures will manage them" (p. 15).

Much of what is readily observed in organizations, according to this analysis, is an organization's "artifacts," that is, "the visible organizational structures and processes," which include "its physical environment, language, technology and products, its style and the organizational processes into which such behavior is made routine" (Schein, 1985, p. 17). This part of an organization is easy to observe but difficult to interpret. In particular, Schein cautions against attempting to infer the meaning of artifacts, since one's own values inevitably are fed into such interpretations. Rather, Schein suggests that the effective analysis must get beyond the artifacts, to two additional levels of culture.

"Espoused values," which are present through the expression of the values of leaders, and initially followed by others as a way to proceed, constitute the first of these additional levels of culture. If these espoused values become effective for the group, in enhancing their work and creating progress toward goals, then the values are transformed in "shared basic assumptions" (Schein, 1985, p. 20). Thus, "when a solution to a problem works repeatedly, it comes to be taken for granted" (p. 21).

In time, people in the organization accept these values so thoroughly that they are no longer confronted, debated, or questioned. Like Thomas Kuhn's (1970) notion of "paradigm," basic assumptions cause individuals to perceive reality so that it is congruent with the assumptions, even if this involves self-delusion. Basic assumptions thus become very difficult to change. It is only through leaders that can, at least temporarily, step outside the prevailing culture that new, innovative approaches can be suggested and tried. This brings us back, of course, to the initial step in organizational culture formation, that of leadership proposals.

Because individuals and groups place a high value on stability, changing an organization's basic assumptions—which is the key to changing its culture—is a very long and difficult process. As Schein (1985) points out, "The most central issue . . . is how to get at the deeper levels of a culture, how to assess the functionality of the assumptions made at each level, and how to deal with the anxiety that is unleashed when those levels are challenged" (p. 27). Many other scholars, as well, have documented the importance of these basic concepts to the process of organizational change. Goldin (1990), in her analysis of women's economic progress, for example, writes that "change is often stymied by institutions, norms, stereotypes, expectations, and other factors that serve to impose the past on the present" (p. 9). Because the gender issues in the workplace examined here are clearly a result of the basic cultures of a variety of work organizations and professions, they highlight the importance of using these ideas to understand the problems at hand, their underlying causes, and potential means for accomplishing change.

Although it is not possible to fully analyze the basic assumptions of each of the organizations included in the cases here, a brief reexamination of the organizations reinforces the importance of organizational culture to the gender issues raised. In "Half a Pie, or None?" there was clearly a basic assumption, at least on the part of a few top managers, that women are inappropriate for the very demanding work of evaluators. The precise reasons for this stereotype were never clearly acknowledged by those who espoused it; nonetheless, because no women held this position, and women continued to be denied access to it, it seems clear that *some* underlying assumption must have been reinforcing the organizational artifact of denying women these positions. Mr. Green's reluctance, despite his personal support of Ms. Andersen, to confront his organization is further evidence that an important underlying value was influencing behavior on this matter.

Students may have identified some possible means of attempting to affect the procedures and other artifacts of the culture that were blocking Ms. Andersen and other women from this work. Schein's contribution, however, would argue that, in addition to attacking the artifacts both within and outside of the organization, through legal action, for instance, leaders committed to solving this problem in a more permanent way would have to challenge the prevailing assumption that is facilitating this behavior. In the case, no leader really appeared willing to take on this challenge, although the new CEO, near the end of the case, indicated that he might do so in the future.

Thus, Mr. Green and Ms. Andersen, throughout the case, had a variety of choices regarding her individual situation; few of these would permanently affect the organization, however, unless basic assumptions in the culture were challenged. Nevertheless, individual actions remain important, because the cumulative impact of many *individual* challenges to the culture may, in time, provide "ammunition" for subsequent leaders to prove to others that the current assumptions are unworkable.

Similarly, Meghan Evans's experience in seeking promotion to partner was fundamentally affected by the organizational culture in her law firm. The espoused values related to the evaluation of the work of associates were reflected in the evaluation forms used by the firm and the comments of the various partners on their evaluations of Ms. Evans's work. Furthermore, the firm espoused thorough evaluation, standardized in form, and at least somewhat quantitative in nature, as its reflection of the value of fairness. The case also makes clear that the firm denied gender bias in both its operating procedures and underlying assumptions.

Not clear, however, is the place of the espoused value of "legal analytical ability" within the firm's value structure. Some of the partners believed that this ability was a sine quo non for partners, an absolute essential, whereas other data in the case, particularly some of the judgments about male associates, indicated that weakness in one legal area might perhaps be compensated for by strength in another. Confusion over this matter contributed to the conflicting judgments of the district court and the appeals court. Ms. Evans's difficulty in establishing gender bias in her evaluation process, after the initial court ruling, reflected the complexity of analyzing the firm's underlying basic assumptions; it was unclear to the appeals court whether systematic gender bias was, as Ms. Evans claimed, a feature of the firm's organizational culture.

In this case, the evaluation process used to select partners was a crucial artifact of the firm's culture, but as Schein's model would suggest, the most essential part of the analysis involves determining the basic assumptions of the firm, which is not possible to do simply using the artifacts. The epilogue's allusion to the number of partners exiting the firm subsequent to this case might suggest dissatisfaction with the firm's prevailing organizational culture, although specific reasons for the unusual number of disaffections are not provided. The suggested analysis (in the Student Response) of the actions that partners and future associates might take in an attempt to improve the organizational climate for women in the firm suggests the importance of individual leaders in promoting change in the culture.

"Medical Mentoring" describes situations of young women physicians that are a direct reflection of the current culture of the medical profession. The long hours worked in medical practices and the necessity of "sponsorship" by elders in the key specialties, in particular, reflect underlying assumptions about what makes a "good" medical practitioner. Another issue raised in the case, the slow rate of advancement of women on medical school faculties, is an important artifact of those institutions and how they determine advancement. It may or may not reflect underlying bias against women in leadership roles in medical schools.

Of particular importance to the sponsorship issue raised in the case is the socialization process through which norms of a specialty are learned. The senior practitioners in the medical specialties served as "gatekeepers," effectively determining who gains admission to a given specialty. Once accepted by a senior practitioner, the young physician learns much about that field of practice, makes important contacts, and so on, as a result of his or her mentoring. The individual values of these gatekeepers then effectively determine who enters the field and what they are taught about its practices. The women in the case, therefore, correctly determined that obtaining such sponsorship was vital to their success. The ultimate power to change the situation, however, clearly rested in the hands of the senior physicians. It is these individuals who would need to confront the prevailing norm of male dominance of the desired specialties, if the overall pattern in the profession is to be changed. Schein's emphasis on the critical role of leaders in changing an organizational culture is thus very relevant to this case.

The discussion of balancing family and professional demands in "Medical Mentoring" suggested that at least some of the satisfied women physicians in the case were successful because they created their own organizations (medical practices) in which they could then define their schedules, volume of work, and so on, by themselves or with a similarly minded partner. This is another option for circumventing a prevailing organizational culture, by creating a new organization. The founders, as Schein's work suggests, have the freedom to impose their own values on the new culture, at least at the outset. When these values prove effective for the organization—as in the case of one of the medical practices described in "Medical Mentoring"— they then become embedded in the organization as its basic assumptions. Thus, Dr. Marcia Birthright and her partner in medical practice appear content with their family-work balance because the two have defined the basic assumptions of the practice to be congruent with their individual values and needs. The increasing numbers of women founding their own businesses indicate the widespread adoption of this independent approach to work among American women.

The principals in "The Pregnant Professor" did not have the luxury of establishing their own organizational culture, however. Karen and Tim needed to find ways to adapt to work organizations that would be compatible with the needs of their marriage and their young child. As the case makes clear, both individuals encountered specific and difficult underlying assumptions in their employing organizations that complicated their lives considerably. For example, Midwest University, at least in Karen's academic department, espoused values of long, isolated periods of work, with professional output of publications very rigidly prescribed. The basic assumptions of Karen's department, according to her subsequent mentor, even conflicted with some of the values and practices being used in other parts of the organization. This points to the importance that the assumptions of *one part* of an organization may have, even if in apparent contradiction with the procedures and espoused values of the organization as a whole.

Both Karen, at Worth College, and Tim, in his first teaching in New York, found that the expectations of the role of college teacher were more demanding and tiring than they had anticipated. Their socialization in these two organizations transmitted a set of values that required more work and energy than they previously realized. A variety of organizational procedures, particularly those related to the granting of tenure and pregnancy leave, embodied the underlying assumptions of the two educational institutions for whom Karen worked. These procedures were important organizational artifacts in Karen's progress toward tenure and her personal desires regarding her family. It is clear that Midwest University subsequently responded to the needs of young professors in changing its "tenure clock" for professors adding children to their families. This change in artifact is probably reflective of a change in underlying assumptions, as well.

The heavy demands of Tim's employing organizations, particularly in terms of hours on the job site and resumption of work immediately after the birth of his child, indicated that those organizations were still rather inflexible in terms of the needs and schedules of young families. The situation faced by these two young professionals is precisely the concern of Friedan in *Beyond Gender*, when she argues that fundamental workplace and economic restructuring are needed for the benefit of American families and communities.

Of all the five cases presented here, "Sexual Harassment in the Army" probably provides the most powerful illustration of the importance of organizational culture to gender issues and their improvement. The studies of harassment conducted by the military in the 1980s, and the attention devoted to the issue by leaders in the Army, suggest that the espoused values of the Army are definitely in opposition to the harassment described in the case. Yet the behavior has persisted. It is most likely that there are basic assumptions operating here, about the nature of effective military discipline and command, for example, that provide a protective "cover" for harassment, despite the attempts of leaders to stamp it out. Years of a male-dominated hierarchy, in which drill sergeants are granted almost total authority, cannot be changed simply by espousing antiharassment values in official policy or even in well-designed training. Until vigorous leaders succeed in convincing the organization that harassment is counterproductive and against important basic values, the behavior is unlikely to be eliminated.

In this regard, of course, the Army is not unique; many contemporary organizations may reflect underlying assumptions that are tolerant of harassing behaviors.

If organizational culture is slow to change, then what is the role of public policy or individual action in combating gender discrimination in the workplace? The actions of government are important in at least two ways. First, government policy "models" the desirable values about gender equity and treatment, whether or not all organizations are actually conforming to these values. Thus, the Glass Ceiling Commission charged the federal government with the obligation of being a "model employer" with regard to eliminating the glass ceiling in government agencies. This symbolic role of government is critical.

Second, government policy provides a basic framework of equity principles to which leaders in organizations and individual employees can appeal for remedy in a specific situation. It is important that Title VII exists; it provides the means for forcing organizations to at least change the artifacts of their culture—their formal procedures—to conform to the law. Of course, the law is only as effective as the willingness of individuals to appeal to it, and the strength of government to enforce it. Many critics of equal employment law have effectively argued that lack of enforcement, for example, seriously weakens legal prohibitions against unequal pay, sexual harassment, and so on.

On the other hand, legal protection has undoubtedly assisted many courageous women, and their male supporters, to change the employment practices of many organizations in the past 30 years.

This raises the importance of the individual in promoting workplace fairness and developing effective means of addressing gender issues at work. If individuals who need policy change or enforcement are unwilling to ask for it, then it will not occur. If leaders in organizations recognize that a practice is unfair or ineffective, they must on occasion be willing to directly confront the organizational culture to that effect. Although individual actions, even those of leaders, do not necessarily "fix" an organization, they cumulatively raise awareness of gender issues and provide individual compensation in many instances for illegal or unfair treatment. The lawsuits filed by Meghan Evans and Kristin Andersen confront the court with actual workplace practices and situations; in adjudicating these cases, the courts eventually arrive at a consensus about standards by which to judge these matters, and at effective means of enforcement.

The case studies are messy. They do not resolve the incorporated gender issues neatly or in a universally popular fashion. The solutions to the problems presented are not clear, and they require not only careful analysis but also the acknowledgment that a variety of perspectives on the same situation may have merit. If the cases have caused the reader to reflect on the nature of gender issues in the workplace, and the multiple causes of these issues, as well as stimulated some creativity in possible approaches to the situations they present, then this short collection has succeeded.

 References

Friedan, B. (1963). *The feminine mystique.* New York: Norton.

Friedan, B. (1997). *Beyond gender: The new politics of work and family.* Baltimore, MD: Johns Hopkins University Press.

Garland, S. (1991, September 2). Commentary: How to keep women managers on the corporate ladder. *Business Week,* p. 64.

Goldin, C. (1990). *Understanding the gender gap: An economic history of American women.* Oxford, UK: Oxford University Press.

Komaromy, M., Bindman, A. B., Haber, R. J., & Sande, M. A. (1993). Sexual harassment in medical training. *New England Journal of Medicine, 328,* 322-326.

Kuhn, T. (1970). *The structure of scientific revolutions* (2nd ed.). Chicago: University of Chicago Press.

Schein, E. (1985). *Organizational culture and leadership.* San Francisco: Jossey-Bass.

About the Author

Jacqueline DeLaat is Professor of Political Science and Leadership at Marietta College in Ohio. The McDonough Leadership program in which she teaches is known nationally for its interdisciplinary and experiential approach to leadership education. Dr. DeLaat holds a BA with high distinction in political science from the University of Iowa, an MA in American politics from the University of Minnesota, and a PhD in public administration from the University of Pittsburgh. For nearly 20 years, Dr. DeLaat has taught political science in small liberal arts institutions, with her major teaching responsibilities being in the areas of public policy, public administration, American politics and institutions, and women and politics. She is known as an enthusiastic teacher, favoring active student projects and a dynamic classroom—including the frequent use of current event projects, case studies, and simulations.

Prior to her teaching career, Dr. DeLaat worked in the Washington, D.C., area for approximately ten years, serving in government and in quasi-governmental organizations in a variety of administrative posts. Her Washington experience has enhanced both her subsequent teaching and research. She has also consulted with several private and governmental organizations on gender issues.

For the past several years, Dr. DeLaat's professional agenda has focused on the development of a series of teaching cases designed to prepare students for gender issues in the contemporary workplace. One of her cases won an award at the meeting of the International Case Study Association in 1995. An additional case was presented at the 1997 conference of the World Association for Case Study Research and Application in Edinburgh, Scotland, and is scheduled for publication in that organization's journal. In addition, at the same meeting

Dr. DeLaat led an interactive workshop of international scholars on the topic of developing case studies on gender issues in the workplace. In the summer of 1997, her work on developing gender cases was supported with a special grant from the American Bar Association's Commission on Justice and Education.